DARRELL WALTRIP
ONE-ON-ONE

If life is really the race the Bible says it is then who better to talk about life than the greatest race-car driver who ever lived? DW has undeniably achieved greatness through his success on the racetrack but out of the spotlight is where his true greatness is found through his profound Christian goodness. But the race is filled with struggles, setbacks and failures, for it is after all a fallen world in which we race. Because of grace, however, all of these hardships become occasions for healing and transcendent joy. This paradox, of victory sometimes coming through what looks like defeat, of healing that comes through pain, has been faithfully lived out in the lives of Darrell and Stevie. It has, fortunately for us, been marvelously portrayed in *Darrell Waltrip One-on-One*.

Michael Card
AUTHOR, *SCRIBBLING IN THE SAND* AND *A FRAGILE STONE*
MUSICIAN AND TEACHER

What you read in these challenging pages will validate the reality of Jesus Christ now living in Darrell and Stevie Waltrip, and of their quest for godliness. It has been my joy over the years to be their pastor and friend, as well as DW's mentor.

When we met at church again recently in Nashville, with the bear hugs as always, DW's eyes were aglow with the prospect of discipling other men; so the race continues, and my trophy case overflows!

Dr. Cortez A. Cooper
PASTOR
DRAPER'S VALLEY, VIRGINIA

Two great storytellers—Darrell Waltrip and Jay Carty—combine their talents to communicate spiritual insights and biblical truths. My heart is uplifted by the messages of these two men in *Darrell Waltrip One-on-One*.

Max Helton

FOUNDER, MOTOR RACING OUTREACH
CEO, WORLD SPAN MINISTRIES

Jay Carty is not only a good writer, he is a gentle giant with a passion for Jesus Christ, young people and anyone who is open to learning the truth about God. He has a knack of getting into the head of some of the world's top athletes, as he does so well here with Darrell Waltrip, NASCAR champion race driver. This book will take you into a world you would not otherwise see. I found *Darrell Waltrip One-on-One* to be a great read!

Tim LaHaye

AUTHOR, LEFT BEHIND SERIES
PASTOR AND SPEAKER

DW is a character off the track and fearless on it. However, he knows what is really important: God and his family. As racers we sometimes think we are the ones who can make anything happen. DW has been on top, and in this book he brings us all—racers and anyone else who has tried to succeed in life—back down to Earth. In these 60 readings we see what is really driving DW. Thanks, Darrell, for showing us how we can all be winners.

Dale Jarrett

NASCAR NEXTEL DRIVER

Stock-car racing is as tough a competition as you'll find anywhere on God's green Earth, and Darrell Waltrip—or DW as we call him—is as tough a competitor as you will find in any sport. On the track, he was relentless. Off the track, there was a point when his life was about to crash. I saw firsthand how God caught DW and transformed him into a champion, not only behind the wheel, but also as a husband, a father, a friend and a man of God. DW holds nothing back in this dynamite devotional. You do not have to be a NASCAR fan to laugh at DW's mistakes, cheer for his victories and be challenged by the great lessons on life in this book. Thanks, DW, for being tough enough and bold enough to tell the truth.

Lake Speed
NASCAR DRIVER

As crazy as it sounds, people often think Darrell is my father or that I am Darrell—and I mercilessly harangue him about it. I am Darrell's younger brother, and as such I have seen the good times and the bad times. I could tell you stories. But the best story of Darrell's life is let loose on the pages of this book. Perfect he is not. Committed, honest and enthusiastic about Jesus he is. If a guy like me can learn stuff about God from his big brother, then everyone can. I think God placed Darrell in the right place at the right time to say the right words. I was blessed by *Darrell Waltrip One-on-One* and I think you will be, too.

Michael Waltrip
NASCAR NEXTEL DRIVER

DARRELL WALTRIP
ONE-ON-ONE

DARRELL WALTRIP
JAY CARTY

Regal

From Gospel Light
Ventura, California, U.S.A.

PUBLISHED BY REGAL BOOKS
FROM GOSPEL LIGHT
VENTURA, CALIFORNIA, U.S.A.
PRINTED IN THE U.S.A.

Regal Books is a ministry of Gospel Light, a Christian publisher dedicated to serving the local church. We believe God's vision for Gospel Light is to provide church leaders with biblical, user-friendly materials that will help them evangelize, disciple and minister to children, youth and families.

It is our prayer that this Regal book will help you discover biblical truth for your own life and help you meet the needs of others. May God richly bless you.

For a free catalog of resources from Regal Books/Gospel Light, please call your Christian supplier or contact us at 1-800-4-GOSPEL *or* www.regalbooks.com.

Cover design by David Griffing
Interior design by Stephen Hahn
Edited by Steven Lawson

All photos courtesy of the Waltrip Collection unless otherwise indicated.

Library of Congress Cataloging-in-Publication Data

Waltrip, Darrell.
 Darrell Waltrip : one-on-one / Darrell Waltrip and Jay Carty.
  p. cm.
 Includes bibliographical references.
 ISBN 0-8307-3463-5
 1. Devotional calendars. I. Carty, Jay. II. Title.
 BV4810.W34 2004
 242'.2—dc22   2004002698

1 2 3 4 5 6 7 8 9 10 11 12 13 14 15 / 10 09 08 07 06 05 04

Rights for publishing this book in other languages are contracted by Gospel Light Worldwide, the international nonprofit ministry of Gospel Light. Gospel Light Worldwide also provides publishing and technical assistance to international publishers dedicated to producing Sunday School and Vacation Bible School curricula and books in the languages of the world. For additional information, visit www.gospellightworldwide.org; write to Gospel Light Worldwide, P.O. Box 3875, Ventura, CA 93006; or send an e-mail to info@gospellightworldwide.org.

DEDICATION

From Darrell Waltrip
to
My dear, sweet wife, Stephanie, the redhead.

I think that God told me, "Don't let her get away," and somehow I
convinced her to marry me. She gave up her dreams to help me pursue
mine. Stevie has now been by my side for 35 years and has been my biggest
cheerleader. She was the first person who ever really believed in me, that I
could actually do what I dreamed of doing—that I could be a successful
NASCAR driver. She has been an angel to many other drivers, too.
She would sit on toolboxes at the track on hot Saturday afternoons
and would keep laps. I would come home exhausted;
she would come home sunburned.

You have to have a great partner in marriage and I have the best.
Thank you, Stevie.

From Jay Carty
to
Gene and Jacqueline Head

Faithful as friends, dependable as servants and steadfast in their faith,
Gene and Jacqueline have maintained the Yes! Ministries mailing list and
have distributed every *Obedient Thoughts* newsletter ever sent out in
nearly 25 years. My debt to them cannot be calculated. Please accept this
dedication as a token of my lasting gratitude and our lasting friendship.

CONTENTS

THE DW I KNOW

BY STEPHANIE "STEVIE" WALTRIP

I would like to say that being married to Darrell Waltrip has always been wonderful and fulfilling, but that would not be true. I would like to say that he was the man of my dreams, but he was not. I would like to say that our relationship has always been so close that when difficulties came, we always faced them together—I cannot say that either. What I can say is that in spite of all of our foolishness and weaknesses, the Lord Jesus Christ met us where we were, took our hands and led us to a better place.

God loves to make us smile, and that is exactly what happens to my heart when I think about DW cowriting a book of devotions. No one in his or her wildest imagination would have pictured Darrell wearing any hat other than a helmet. The Bible declares, "God chose the foolish things of the world to shame the wise; God chose the weak things of the world to shame the strong. He chose the lowly things of this world and the despised things— and the things that are not—to nullify the things that are" (1 Cor. 1:27-28, *NIV*). God has demonstrated His willingness and faithfulness to fulfill this promise in one very unlikely candidate: Number 17, Darrell Waltrip.

Darrell knew all about God; He just didn't know God. When he was growing up, his parents took him to church and Sunday School regularly. In fact, he was baptized three times! He went to Vacation Bible School and all sorts of special meetings, yet Christ really had no significance in his life.

When I met Darrell, he was young, handsome, funny, clever and consumed with becoming someone who, from his perspective, had value. He did not come from an influential background or family; in fact, it was just the opposite: Darrell's parents were focused on working so that five children could be clothed, fed and housed. There were no extras. Darrell felt that he had to earn his worth, which came in the form of money, position, fame and personal glory. He was the one who had to make it all happen.

Many times during our first 10 years of marriage, we both wondered if marrying each other had been a mistake. Outwardly, we looked like a happy young couple working together to accomplish Darrell's dream and goals; but in private, our relationship was not what either one of us wanted it to be. Darrell was focused on his career and making himself happy; I was focused on Darrell and trying to make him happy. Even though we were together most of the time, each of us was alone. Darrell was so driven to accomplish self-imposed goals and acquire self-worth that he couldn't feel or see the emptiness and futility of the path he'd chosen for himself. I was so focused on him that I could not see my own needs, much less how to have them fulfilled.

On our tenth wedding anniversary, we renewed our vows. I wrote Darrell a note telling him that I loved him more than anything but that I wanted to love God more than him. Change was my heart's desire.

It was at this point that our lives began to move in a more positive direction. My relationship with Christ became more defined, more purposeful. I had a tremendous appreciation for what the Lord had done for me, and I was consumed with a longing to know Him more. The more I learned, the more I shared with Darrell. The closer I got to the Lord, the more influence the Lord through me had on Darrell. I joined Bible Study Fellowship and studied the Bible for the first time. I read my lessons out loud to DW as we traveled to the races. I listened to audiocassettes of sermons from Chuck Swindoll, and so did Darrell, while he was shaving, because I would turn the volume high enough so that he would have to hear them, too.

We began going to a Wednesday night Bible study at Christ Presbyterian Church. It was at one of those studies, in 1983, that Dr. Cortez Cooper asked whether anyone would like to pray to receive Christ or to rededicate himself or herself to Him. Darrell knew then how badly he needed Jesus. Jesus, knowing all of Darrell's sins—yours and mine as well—said to DW's repentant heart, "Here I am! I stand at the door and knock. If anyone hears my voice and opens the door, I will come in and eat with him, and he with me" (Rev. 3:20, *NIV*). Darrell invited this gentle Jesus in, and that is when our journey as real partners began. Unspoken longings, even longings that were deep within my heart that I was unaware of, began to unfold.

There were so many firsts that we shared as a husband and wife. Instead of living life parallel but separate from each other, we became a team. We began listening to Michael Card, a Christian music artist and teacher, and became huge fans. We began praying together and asking the Lord to bless us with children. We'd been trying for years to have children, but with no success. We helped start Motor Racing Outreach in NASCAR. I'd been praying with another couple for Darrell to become involved in a Bible study, and in 1985 local businessmen began meeting in our home every Tuesday morning for an hour of prayer and Bible teaching. Twenty years later, the Bible study is still going strong.

I do not want to give the impression that every part of our lives that was out of place fell into place. Some of our most painful experiences came after Darrell gave his heart to the Lord. For instance, we lost the baby for whom we had waited so long, but we faced the grief together. We have since been given two precious daughters—the first one coming after 18 years of marriage and the second one 5 years later.

Darrell had a very serious accident in 1990 that left him hospitalized for a week and out of racing for a while. He approached this setback with the same gusto with which he raced. Instead of the rehab process taking six months, as originally expected, the Lord healed Darrell's broken arm, enabling him to rehab much faster. Also, at this time Darrell determined not to drink any alcohol. He found during this rehab experience that he was better off without alcohol, and he wanted to be a good role model for his children.

Second Corinthians 5:17 declares, "If anyone is in Christ, he is a new creation; the old has gone, the new has come!" I see evidence of this truth every day in my husband. His life now reflects Jesus' heart in so many areas. Through my relationship with DW, I have learned so many things about Jesus that I would have missed had we given up in those early years.

Every day I see a man in the process of learning to live like Christ, not because he has to, but because he wants to. I have a husband who now gives wise counsel and is a wonderful listener. He is very compassionate and has a grateful heart for all the good things the Lord has given us. His trust in and reliance on the Lord are evident now when life offers pain and setbacks. He is the dearest person God could have given me. His experiences in life— the good and the not so good, on and off the racetrack—have given him a lot from which he can draw and a lot of areas that needed Christ to touch and transform. He has learned that he cannot do anything by himself. He was an "I" guy but now he has learned there's no "I" in "team," and our family is a team. Very seldom does he make a decision now without asking my thoughts, applying what the Bible says and praying. He approaches life with passion and a great sense of humor, which will make for some enjoyable and insightful reading.

Darrell still gets annoyed and sometimes frustrated, but this doesn't happen as often. His intensity and passion are still a part of his personality but they are channeled in a different direction. Today, self-control is a big part of who Darrell is off the track. Before, Darrell was led by his emotions with no forethought to the consequences that could follow. Racing is a very emotional sport with tremendous highs and tremendous lows. Winning meant everything to Darrell and losing had no value. But with Christ, his perspective has changed dramatically. Now Darrell sees God's purpose and love in all our discouraging, lonely and hurtful trappings of life. Seeking the Lord as his refuge, he invites the Lord in to all areas of life. He wants to see who the Lord is and wants to know His purpose in everything, from the disappointments and pain to the successes and fame.

DW is not perfect (and like all of us, never will be); but when I ponder the Lord's new creation in him, my heart rejoices that He has done so much more than all that I could have asked or imagined. My desire is that as you read these pages, you will be encouraged by what the Lord has done in Darrell's life and can see what He can do in yours.

Always a couple. Darrell and Stevie in the early years (above) and renewing their wedding vows (right).

ACKNOWLEDGMENTS

From Darrell Waltrip to

Dr. Cortez Cooper
You led me back to the Lord and helped me get my life
on the right track.

Bill France
Who was always an inspiration to me.

My wife, Stephanie; my daughters, Jessica and Sarah; my parents,
Margaret and Leroy; Carolyn, Bobby, Connie and Michael
(sometimes known as Mikey) and my entire family. You have
sacrificed so much so that I could pursue my dream.

Ken Cope
You have helped Stevie and me in our marriage—
you have taught us how to communicate!

Max Helton, thanks for leading Motor Sports Outreach; Van
Colley; Leonard Isaac; Ed, Smitty and Jerry, you have served me so
well through the years; Rooster and Bubba Alexander, we have
been together for 25 years and I feel like I have adopted you;
Junior Johnson, one of the brightest minds in NASCAR; Rick
Hendricks and all of the others who have helped and encouraged
me through the years. (I know there are so many more!)

Dale Earnhardt
I don't know if you inspired me or drove me, but
you always made me better.

From Jay Carty to

Sam Talbert
(my Paul)
You have discipled me, stood by me, picked me up and helped
guide me for almost 35 years. Thanks again for making sure
the verses we chose were appropriate to the lessons
we wanted to teach.

Special thanks to Marcia Zimmermann who transcribed the
audiocassettes after saving them from the brink of
destruction. Marcia, you are the unsung hero of this production.
You da' ma'am!

*Two people can accomplish more than twice as much as one; they get a
better return for their labor. If one person falls, the other can reach out and
help. But people who are alone when they fall are in real trouble.*
Ecclesiastes 4:9-10

From DW and Jay to

Bill Greig III (our publisher), Steven Lawson (our editor),
David Griffing (our cover designer)
and the entire Regal team

Thank you, Bill, for believing in the One-on-One series. You've
been a great encouragement. Thank you, Steve, for the firm give-
and-take. Your gentle scalpel had a perfect result. David, the cover
is exceptional. Thank you to the entire Regal team—you form the
perfect blend of friendly professionals.

INTRODUCTION

BOOGITY, BOOGITY, BOOGITY

BY JAY CARTY

I was speaking to a small group of motor sports professionals. Present were boat, drag and short-track dirt racers, some of the guys who worked in the pits, three big-time Winston Cup drivers and a few spouses. My job for the weekend was to bring spiritual refreshment and some laughs.

Darrell Waltrip arrived late for one of the meetings, so I got after him a bit—just for fun. We exchanged a few good-natured barbs. Being 6-foot-8 and commanding a strong voice, I usually had no problem intimidating would-be hecklers. Waltrip, however, didn't flinch. Later, I asked him about my inability to daunt him. In his down-home Southern drawl, he responded, "Oh, I dunno, Jay. Maybe it's doin' a hunnard and eighty miles an hour, two inches from the wall." With this, we connected, but it would be several years before the opportunity came to team up in writing this book.

Born Darrell Lee Waltrip on February 5, 1947, in Owensboro, Kentucky, he goes by the handle DW. Most of the other racers call him by his initials, and I have caught myself occasionally calling him D Dub. As you read and get to know him, you probably will, too. That is fine—DW does not seem to mind.

DW began driving professionally in 1966, started Winston Cup racing in 1972 and won three championships (1981, 1982 and 1985). He amassed 84 Winston Cup wins (third all-time), 59 pole positions and was the National Association for Stock Car Auto Racing (NASCAR) Driver of the Decade (1980s).

To get an idea of how good Darrell Waltrip was behind the wheel, we need to understand at least a little about auto racing. We can use the levels of professional baseball to better grasp the pecking order of various venues under the NASCAR umbrella. The Nextel Cup competition (called the Winston Cup before 2004) is the equivalent of the major leagues. The Busch Series compares to triple A. The Craftsman Truck series corresponds with double A. Short tracks of one-quarter to one-half mile and dirt tracks parallel Triple-A ball. Indy and Formula One cars are a different breed all together. They don't qualify as stock cars.

Stock-car racing has long been the biggest thing going in the South, but more recently NASCAR has boomed all over the United States. One reason for this success is coverage on Fox Sports and the insight of Darrell Waltrip, who has successfully gone from competing on the track to analyzing in the television booth. Chris Ballard wrote in *Sports Illustrated* about Waltrip the announcer: "Racing fans call him a combination of John Madden, Terry Bradshaw and Charles Barkley all rolled into one, a folksy, down-home guy who always tells it like it is."[1] Waltrip's signature call of "Boogity, boogity, boogity" at the beginning of races has made "Gentlemen, start your engines" obsolete.

DW and his wife, Stevie, form an unlikely couple. She graduated cum laude from Vanderbilt University. Darrell says, "Stevie brings book smarts to the table. I bring the street smarts. It's a great combination." Her father was a Harvard attorney. Darrell's ambition went no further than being with Stevie and becoming the best at driving a race car; plus he was a little wild and everybody knew it. As a high school kid, he had actually led a *Smokey-and-the-Bandit*-type chase involving close to 30 police cars. In spite of his antics, DW made it through high school and avoided jail, but college wasn't his bag. There was driving to do.

Stevie's dad did everything he could to keep her away from DW, including sending her to Hawaii and faking a heart attack—but to no avail. The pair became the Waltrips, scrounged and lived on credit while Darrell got his start and caught a couple of breaks, and the rest is history. DW's dad had taught him how to work hard; Stevie's dad—who finally accepted his son-in-law—taught him the art of business, and the good Lord provided the instincts and aptitudes to be the best. DW did the rest.

When I flew to Tennessee to spend some concentrated time with Darrell to work on this book, I sensed that cornering him would be like herding cats. I realized he was a busy guy and full of energy. We had a long list of points we needed to cover. My work was cut out for me because there was a party DW and Stevie *had* to attend, a football game to catch and a trip to the lake house that was a fixed commitment. Plus there were business matters that needed DW's attention. Given this, it was a challenge to go one-on-one in the midst of such a demanding personal schedule. It's a good thing that DW can think and talk nearly as fast he drives.

The Waltrips have been married for 34 years. They tried to have children for 18 of those years. The Lord finally gave them two wonderful, beautiful and charming daughters. At 56 years of age, DW is father to a 16-year-old and an 11-year-old. Jessica, the eldest, is very much like her mother: confident and extremely intelligent. Sarah is charismatic, captivating and very dramatic. She has her father's skills with people and words—and I would not be surprised if one day she wins an Academy Award. I won't soon forget her rendition of Scarlet O'Hara as she turned, standing in the doorway, dramatically playing the role on her way out the door to the patio.

Stevie homeschools the girls—and DW helps when he can. They all take care of four dogs and a cat. Darrell goes nonstop. When he's not watching the Speed Channel or Fox Sports, he is constantly receiving calls on his cell phone. In the evening, the family usually goes out to eat. Afterward, when it's a special occasion, they hit Maggie Moos for ice cream. It was special two of the four nights I was there, and I was three pounds heavier by the time I got home.

Darrell Waltrip is a charismatic master of one-liners as the spokesman for NASCAR on Fox television, owns a truck that he sometimes drives in the Craftsman truck series, has Honda and Volvo dealerships in Franklin, Tennessee, hosts a Tuesday-morning Bible study for 80 guys in his garage and, with Stevie, was one of the founders of Motor Sports Outreach. DW knows the art of racing inside out, and he loves God. I found him to be approachable, outgoing, articulate and tons of fun. Quite honestly, I've never met anyone quite like him.

I hope you enjoy this peek inside the world and the faith of arguably one of the five greatest race-car drivers of all time. Buckle up as you begin your day going one-on-one with DW. In each of the 60 readings, Darrell starts with a story or an observation about life or a lesson he has learned. Then it is my turn, and you'll go one-on-one with me. On the page opposite DW's page, I expand upon the point of the day, using either Scripture or one of my own experiences. While I have never driven a stock car, I promise to keep you on track, riding on rails, not too tight and not too loose, on your way to taking the checkereds. Finally, before we finish each reading, you can go one-on-one with God by talking to Him in prayer and letting Him talk to you as you read a few suggested Bible verses.

DW and I pray that when you have completed 60 laps going one-on-one, you will spend the rest of your life in Victory Circle and that you'll be ready to cut doughnuts and burn the hides in heaven for eternity. For anyone who does not speak NASCARese, this simply means you'll be a champion and have a great time with God!

A fierce competitor. DW behind the wheel. Boogity, boogity, boogity.

© CIA Stock Photo

WALTRIP CARTY

ONE-ON-ONE

Worth the Wreck?

It is pleasant to see dreams come true, but fools will not turn from evil to attain them.

PROVERBS 13:19

We were in the final lap of the Winston All-Star Race at the Charlotte Speedway. The year was 1995. I had drafted off of Jeff Gordon and went high on the track to try to pass. I looked to my left and saw Dale Earnhardt drop in on the low side. We were going into the third turn three wide—Jeff, Dale and me. That's fine if you're at Talladega. That track is wide enough. But it's not so fine at Charlotte. It's narrower there. Of the three of us, whoever didn't wreck would win the race.

You need to know that Dale and I were what I call "frienemies." Off the track, we were friends. Our motor coaches were parked next to each other's. But on the track, I would rather wreck than let him win. He felt exactly the same way about me. Who would lift (his foot off the gas pedal)? That was the question. I knew that Dale wouldn't. He knew that I wouldn't. Jeff knew that neither of us would, so he lifted, assuming Dale and I would crash each other.

My eyes met Dale's eyes for a split second. Volumes were communicated in that moment without saying a word.

Are you gonna lift?

No way! Are you?

No!

Let's wreck.

So we did. Dale's front left tire bit into the apron as he drifted too low. When the chassis's weight transferred, his vehicle shot up the track. Jeff had pulled out just in time. Dale's car crashed into mine and took us both into the wall. As crazy as it sounds, even though we were doing over 180 miles an hour, we chose to wreck. I broke three ribs, and Jeff Gordon went low, got through and won the race. Dale and I were so set against each other that we lost sight of the bigger picture and the consequences of our actions.

–DW

There once was a big pig on a farm in Oregon that was a lot like DW and Dale. This pig was standing at a gate, but the opening was narrower than the hog was wide and the posts on each side were charged with electricity. The porker had been through this gate before and knew the electrifying consequences, so it stood and pondered the options.

The consideration was how long to delay the pain, not whether to inflict it. The mud on the other side was just too desirable. Finally, the curly-tailed oinker began to squeal. The sound rose to a feverish pitch as the pig imitated a dragster at the line revving its engine as the starting lights begin their descent from red to green. The animal tensed, dashed, got zapped and didn't stop squealing until it jumped in the mud.

We are a lot like this pig. We decide to sin and start hollering about the consequences even before we do it. We show remorse over the backlash of adultery on our spouse and children before having an affair, and then we do it anyway. We overspend, knowing full well the cost after the purchase will be greater than the actual price paid. We gossip, knowing the repercussions of our words will last longer than the feeling of being a big shot. It's the same with an addiction, whether it involves nicotine, alcohol, drugs, pornography or food. We lament the consequences, scream and dash through the gate not realizing that, unlike the pig, the zapping can last for the rest of our lives.

Just like the pig thought the mud bath was worth the pain, DW and Dale thought keeping the other guy from winning would be worth the wreck. However, DW lost more than a race. His broken ribs took him out of the point standings that year and started a downward spiral that would become the most difficult period of his life.

In the spiritual realm, sin only takes a moment, but it starts a downward spiral of consequences that last forever. What seems a good idea at the time pales in the light of eternity. Sin is not worth it. Don't get zapped. Don't wreck. Finish the race.

–JC

Holy caring and forgiving Shepherd, I don't want to dishonor Your name. I don't want to wreck again. Please heal me from the times I crashed in the past. Give me the courage to stay out of the mud. And forgive me for the times I got in. Thank You.

TODAY'S READING: 2 THESSALONIANS 2:11-12; JOHN 3:16-21; ECCLESIASTES 7:29; 2 PETER 2:22; PROVERBS 13:19

From Frienemies to Friends

And do not bring sorrow to God's Holy Spirit by the way you live. Remember, he is the one who has identified you as his own, guaranteeing that you will be saved on the day of redemption.

EPHESIANS 4:30

I kept my car at Dale Earnhardt's father-in-law's place, and I knew Dale from day one. When he was in his early 20s, he was a chip off the old block. A rough rednecked kid, he drove dirt tracks just like his dad had done. Looking at him, no one would have guessed that he would have the kind of success he eventually had.

He was three years younger than I was; and even though we started out as friends, it did not stay that way. As time went by, a lot of tension grew between us. I was envious of Richard Petty when I started racing because he was the king of the hill and had what I wanted. In the 1980s, Dale was jealous of me because I had what he wanted. He raced me harder than anyone else; he even wrecked me a couple of times. I always tried to get him back. Sometimes we were friends. Sometimes we were enemies. We were frienemies.

In 1986, at Richmond, Dale wrecked me and almost killed me. He slammed my car through the fence. When we wrecked at Charlotte in 1995, I broke my ribs and my run ended.

For many years I owned my own race team. In 1998, I sold it but was obligated to drive for the new owner. Dale called and wanted me to drive for his team instead. He had spent millions on a new facility, but he had eight wrecked race cars and a driver who was hospitalized. Plus, Pennzoil, his sponsor, was very concerned. This was an opportunity to heal my relationship with Dale, race in a good car, be on a good team and not have the pressure of being an owner—but I already had a commitment. The next day, out of nowhere, the new owner called and released me from that commitment. The next day! In my mind, it was a real God thing.

I was glad to help Dale and he was glad to help me. God used us to help each other. Pennzoil continued as his sponsor and I got to keep racing. Dale and I worked through our stuff, and we moved from being frienemies to being friends again.

—DW

Sin makes us frienemies with God. It took a dramatic act to bridge the gap so that we can be friends with Him. In fact, it was our sin that sent Christ to the cross. Our basic nature is another frienemy. It too is dangerous, because our willingness to continue in sin wrecks our fellowship with God.

Ananias and Sapphira are examples of what can happen when we are freinemies with God. Their hearts weren't pure, and they were dangerous. They were trying to use the church for their benefit. They didn't care if anybody else wrecked, and they didn't care about God.

A and S were at the Pearl Direct level with ShackWayLife and enjoyed being in a big church because of all the contacts. Peter's church was booming.

The couple sold a piece of property, brought part of the money and gave it to the elders. They said they had given the total proceeds, when actually they had only given a portion. God didn't care if they gave all or part. What He did care about was their act of lying and why they lied. God told Peter, and Pete sent for Ananias.

Ananias was pleased when he walked in. All the elders were there, along with Peter. *I'm finally in the inner circle*, he surely thought. Then Ananias's attention turned to Matthew. *I'll bet he's about ready to attend a ShackWayLife meeting. With his contacts, he could become a Direct in no time. Sapphira and I will be at Emerald Direct before we know it.*

Then Peter told him what he'd done,[1] and before Ananias could start smooth talking, God dropped him like a rock. When Sapphira came in, He did the same thing to her.[2] They would never make Diamond Direct.

Word of the two deaths traveled fast on the prayer chain. Everyone realized just how serious God was about their having pure hearts, and they concluded that it was dumb to try and snow Him. Not even becoming a Triple Diamond in ShackWayLife was worth the risk.

We have to confess and repent in order to stop being frienemies with God. We must come clean with our sin and stop doing it. Our heavenly Father wants us to have pure hearts so that we can go from being His frienemies to being His friends.

–*JC*

Heavenly Father, I confess my sin. Forgive me. I repent. My desire is to turn from sin to You. Show me the hidden stuff that I might confess and repent of it, too. Thank You. Amen.

TODAY'S READING: ACTS 5:1-11; COLOSSIANS 3:1-17; 1 THESSALONIANS 5:12-22

Duct Tape and the Word

The name of the LORD is a strong tower;
the righteous run to it and are safe.

PROVERBS 18:10, NKJV

Before each race, my wife, Stevie, would pray and ask God for the right Scripture for me for that day. She would then write it on a note card or a hunk of duct tape and give it to me as I got in the car. At some point she started giving a verse to Dale Earnhardt, too. Stevie tells the story.

One day I was out on pit road with a roll of gray duct tape, and I was writing on it. This was right before the race started. Dale walked by. We were just acquaintances, even though we'd been around the same racetracks for years. He stopped and asked me what I was doing. I told him and he said, "Where's mine?" It was his way.

From that day on, Dale didn't want to race until he had his Scripture. When DW and Dale were both racing, Dale would take both verses I had written out, pick the one he wanted and give the other one to Darrell. He would always look at me and say, "I got the best one, didn't I?" That was his way.

I signed each verse with "I love you." When I wasn't there, Darrell would give the verse to Dale. Sometimes Darrell would sign it "I love you, Stevie." Sometimes he signed it "I love you, Darrell." If it didn't say, "I love you," Dale made Darrell add the words.

On the day Dale died, I had prayed intently about the verse I should give him. I was late getting to pit road with Dale's Scripture. Dale was nervously looking for me, but smiled warmly when I arrived. He read the verse, thanked me, stuck it on his dash and drove off.

Dale always raced for himself, but not that day. Dale backed off and blocked for the two front-runners, his racing teammates, Michael Waltrip and his son, Dale, Jr. That's what he was doing on the last half of the last lap when he hit the wall the last time—head-on at almost 180 miles an hour—with his verse on his dash.

I had seen enough changes in Dale over the years that I'm convinced God gave me his last Scripture so that I, and everyone else who cared about him, might be comforted as to the condition of his soul. This Scripture must have applied to Dale's life. Why else would God have given it to me on that day? The Scripture I gave him was "The name of the Lord is a strong tower; the righteous run to it and are safe."

—DW

The word "safe" in Hebrew means "inaccessibly high, secure and out of danger." A safe place was far enough within the outer walls and was high enough to be secure even from arrows. A strong tower was safe.

Before the race. Stevie gives Dale a hand-picked Scripture.

The word "righteous" doesn't mean "good." It means "forgiven."

"The Lord" means "Jesus Christ." So, when the righteous run into the strong tower, the verse actually means "the forgiven are already in a strong tower." Christ is the place where the forgiven are secure.

Salvation is the ultimate strong tower. It is what the Old Testament refers to in "My God is my rock, in whom I find protection. He is my shield, the strength of my salvation, and my stronghold, my high tower, my savior."[1]

Stevie Waltrip believes Dale Earnhardt's reliance on Scripture went from initially being a lucky charm or rabbit's foot, to a dependence on the Strong Tower into which he drove. Stevie told me, "Dale was drawn to the Scripture, he reverenced it, and he blocked out everything else while he read it." Other verses she had given him had covered the role of Jesus Christ as Savior. He had dwelled on them as well.

Dale knew God's plan. Stevie Waltrip had made sure of that. She believes the final verse was given by God to comfort Dale's loved ones and her. Stevie believes Dale Earnhardt entered into his Strong Tower on February 18, 2001, when the number 3 car hit the wall at Daytona.

Are you ready to enter your Strong Tower?

–GC

Holy God, I acknowledge Your name as my Strong Tower. Thank You for the assurance of my salvation. Amen.

TODAY'S READING: PROVERBS 18:10; 2 SAMUEL 22:3; PSALM 18:2; PSALM 61:3

Good-Bye Superman

Godly men buried Stephen and mourned deeply for him.

ACTS 8:2, *NIV*

You never expect anyone to get killed. Every Sunday in a race somebody could crash and die, but you just don't anticipate it. Dale Earnhardt had been in a million wrecks. He had hit the wall and he had turned over. He was like Superman. He was Earnhardt. He always got up and raced again. He was too tough to get killed at a racetrack. He might kill a race car, but there was no race car that would kill him.

For me, Dale's death was so huge because I was there, but I wasn't in the race. It was the first time we hadn't been on the racetrack together. He was in a car; I was in a broadcast booth. So, it was different.

This was my brother Michael's first race for the Earnhardt team. He hadn't won a Winston Cup race yet. But on the last lap, Michael was going to win the Daytona 500, Dale, Jr. was going to run second, Dale, Sr. was going to finish third. Dale, Sr. was going to be in Victory Circle, he was going to have his arm around his son and my brother, and he was going to tell people, "I told you these guys could drive." It was going to be his payoff.

It's ironic that he got killed blocking for his teammates. He wasn't even trying to win the race, which meant he was doing something totally uncharacteristic and unexpected. Then he got killed.

When I arrived at the hospital, everybody was stunned. Superman was dead.

On Thursday, at the memorial service, it was rainy, windy and cold—it was miserable but moving. We remembered, and then we left for the next race at Rockingham. That's the way it works. That's the way Dale, Sr. would have wanted it.

When I got to Rockingham, in the spot where Dale always parked his coach, there was a wreath. I almost went home. I almost said, "I can't do this." It was so—unbelievable. Superman was dead.

Dale, Sr. and I had made a lot of sparks over the years. I doubt that he ever realized the place he held in our hearts or how much Stevie and I would miss him. I think we are still grieving. I know we are.

—DW

At some time in our lives we all lose someone close to us. It is particularly hard when that person was the one whom God used to sharpen our rough edges—like iron sharpening iron.[1] DW lost a good friend when Dale's car slammed into a wall. I lost a good friend when his plane slammed into a mountain. Like DW, some of my iron is gone.

Dave Sundquist was a traveling preacher. He was my Superman, and he was iron in my life. We rubbed on each other. Dave helped improve both my ministry and my marriage. But I lost him and his wife in a plane crash. I was happy for them.

Yes, I was happy. Think about it. They flew into the arms of God together. Neither one had to grieve the other's passing. That is as good as it gets. But I suffered great loss and I grieved a lot. Even now, I still miss my iron.

Time has helped lessen the pain and decrease the sadness. But it took so long, and I felt so badly. I wanted patience, and I wanted it right then! I wanted the time to pass quickly so that I wouldn't hurt so much—but it didn't. It's better now because God has filled part of the void—but not all. Time and God have helped with the pain and sadness, but the loss has never quite gone away. There is still a little empty place.

As I talked with DW and Stevie, even after almost three years, their eyes still moistened as they told their stories about their friend Dale Earnhardt. A tremble came upon their lips and there was a quiver in their voices. They weren't over their loss either.

Jacob tore his clothes and put on sackcloth when he mourned the loss of his son.[2] Jesus wept at the news of the death of Lazarus, even though He knew His friend would only be down for four days.[3] And godly men mourned the death of Stephen.[4] In both the Old and New Testaments, mourning is expected, so it's okay to weep and grieve when you lose someone dear to you. In time, God will fill most of the void—but not all. You will always have an empty place where your iron used to be.

—GC

Holy Comforter, console us in our losses. Help us to bear up under the pain. Bring us joy in the midst of sadness, and remind us to reflect the image of Christ in all that we must endure. May You be glorified. Amen.

TODAY'S READING: PSALM 42:5-8; PROVERBS 27:17; MATTHEW 5:4; ACTS 7:54—8:2; ROMANS 8:28; HEBREWS 4:14-16

All in the Family

*God blessed them and told them, "Multiply and
fill the earth and subdue it."*

GENESIS 1:28

Mom worked at the IGA market all day long. Dad drove a Dr. Pepper truck. He'd leave early and come back late, so we didn't have a lot of family life. There were five kids. For our big family treat, Mom would pop a grocery bag full of popcorn and we'd get some Dr. Pepper; then we'd jump in the car and go to the drive-in. Or we'd go to Wendell's Wonder Whip and get a Wonder Burger. That was special, too.

Sundays we went to church, and sometimes we'd go on Wednesday nights for a prayer meeting. Occasionally we'd go on Thursday nights, because that was visitation night, when we'd go around and visit people. We'd ask them to come to church and we'd pray for them.

I slept in the same bed with my brother Bobby. Connie and Carolyn had a room together. Mom and Dad had their bedroom. When my youngest brother Michael came along, we had nowhere for him to go, so we had to improvise. Dad moved the washer and dryer into the storage room and built Michael a bunk bed. We had seven people living in a little bitty house. It was packed, and I couldn't wait to get out when I was old enough. I'd spend as many nights as I could at various friends' houses.

For a really big family deal, we would drive to Henderson, Kentucky, and spend a weekend with my aunt and uncle. Picture this: There were seven of us, and we'd spend a weekend with a family that had 12 kids. They had a big house and we'd sleep everywhere. We would dig a pit in the ground and have a barbeque. We would cook chickens and mutton, and in 50-gallon kettles we made a kind of Brunswick stew called burgoo. Mutton and burgoo are Western Kentucky things.

We loved spending weekends at one of the aunt's houses. Aunt Emma had 12 kids, Aunt Edna had 12, and Aunt Clarice had like 8 or 9. We'd also do a family reunion once a year at Aunt Rina's. There'd probably be 75 to 100 of us for a weekend. When God said "multiply and fill the earth," the Waltrips took Him seriously!

–DW

Jesus had a big family, too. We assume that He had four half brothers and at least three half sisters. Note that His siblings were only "half." In Hawaiian, that's *happa*, or *halfa*. Jesus was happa. He wasn't a product of Joseph's loins. The others were.

In that day, the law required that all Jewish males who lived within 20 miles of Jerusalem attend temple three times a year—at Passover, Pentecost and the Feast of Tabernacles.[1] Women could go, but they didn't have to. Both Joseph and Mary went every year which means that they worshiped by choice, not by law, and that they loved God. For Jesus, a trip to Jerusalem must have been like going for a Wonder Burger at Wendell's Wonder Whip. Here is why.

At 13, a Jewish boy was considered a man and was expected to keep the Law. It was the custom for all who could hear with understanding to be present in Temple if at all possible.[2] That meant that 11- and 12-year-olds were encouraged to come so that they could become familiar with Temple traditions and practices.

On one trip, Jesus went with his parents to Jerusalem. Joseph and Mary must have been doing separate errands or something because when they got back together they went through the classic, I-thought-Jesus-was-with-you-No-honey-I-thought-He-was-with-you routine.

Their 12-year-old son was found three days later in the midst of the teachers. The better word is "doctors," meaning Ph.D.s of religion. The doctors who would have been there included Gamaliel, who taught Paul, or Saul of Tarsus; Hillel, a raging liberal; Shammai, a revered conservative; Jonathan, who paraphrased the sacred books; Simeon, who would succeed Hillel; and Nicodemus, who later talked to Jesus alone. Jesus held His own with these guys. No wonder everyone was amazed.

Joseph died early on, but we don't know when. It's likely that Jesus had been the head of the household for some time before he started his public ministry. Two of His early miracles were at gatherings. I wonder, if Jesus had been born in Western Kentucky, would He have turned water into moonshine or multiplied the mutton and burgoo instead of the fishes and loaves?

One day we will be part of a great reunion. It will be the party to end all parties. Everyone who has ever loved the Son of God will be there. Y'all come now, ya hear?

–*GC*

Heavenly Father, thank You for my family and for the people You have put in my life to love me. Thank You that I can experience Your perfect love, even when love in this life is less than perfect. I love You, Lord.

TODAY'S READING: LUKE 2:41-51; DEUTERONOMY 6:7;
PROVERBS 22:6; PSALMS 34:11; 119:99-100

Growing up fast. DW quickly graduated from a wagon with puppies (left) to a go-kart (above). He even gave tips to little brother, Michael (below).

Hot wheels. DW shows off one of his first race cars (above) and his number 88 Gatorade car (below).

From Go-Karts to NASCAR

Before I formed you in the womb I knew you, before you were born I set you apart; I appointed you as a prophet to the nations.

JEREMIAH 1:5, *NIV*

I'd been going to dirt-track races with my granny since I was six years old, so I was into racing. I read *Hot Rod* magazine and everything I could get my hands on about cars. I had a dream. I didn't want to be a doctor or a fireman—I wanted to be a racer. One problem: We barely got by, and I had no idea how I would ever get behind the wheel of a race car. My dad loved us boys, and he was wise enough to see what we could be good at. So he took a risk and found a way to get me started.

I was helping Daddy on his Dr. Pepper truck one summer day. We went into West End Hardware and the owner was unloading go-karts. I was fascinated.

The bossman said, "Get on that thing!"

I sat down on it, and he fired up the engine. It was running, and I was dreaming about winning a trophy. I said, "Dad, we've got to get us one of these."

My daddy made about $100 a week for all of us to live on. The go-kart cost $300! I devised a plan on the spot. We would buy the go-kart and a power lawn mower. I could work it off mowing lawns. The salesman could see that I wanted the go-kart, so he worked with us. I had to make payments, something like $10 a month.

We drove up our driveway with this shiny, nice, beautiful go-kart sticking out of the trunk. We unloaded that thing, and we're proud as peacocks. *Man. Look what we got!* I thought my mother was gonna kill my dad and me. She flipped out, but after a lot of hollerin' and yellin', Daddy told her that we couldn't take it back. So we kept it.

On Sunday, we went to church with the go-kart sticking out of the trunk. Bless her heart, mama had fried up chicken and fixed a picnic lunch. After church the whole family went to the Fashion Fair parking lot, and we raced the go-kart—and that's how I became a race-car driver.

—DW

Each of us carries a treasure in our earthen vessel. God designed these riches to be discovered and displayed to reveal His glory."[1] Hawaiian pastor Wayne Cordeiro penned these words in his book about how we can help others release their dreams. I call this discovering our natural talents.[2] God has gifted each of us for excellence. Our task is to unearth our areas of natural talent and unleash them to the best of our ability and to the fullest of our potential.

That's not always easy. Sometimes parents want their children to become what they never became, or they want them to follow in their footsteps. Neither goal takes into account the natural talents of their children. Sometimes our talent mix may not be suited to something that pays well or is glamorous. Our educational system emphasizes reading, writing and arithmetic. Music and art are pass/fail classes and drama is an after-school club. Those with talents outside of the big three are rarely validated in school and, as a result, may not pursue their strongest suit. In fact, many people reach middle age with that uneasy feeling that they never did what they were wired to do.

As financially strapped as the Waltrips were, Darrell's dad saw something in his son that needed to be developed, and he helped move mountains to make it happen. In biblical terms, DW became wise. With his dad's support, he took his God-given talents to the A+ level, and that was good enough to make him one of the best drivers who ever got behind the wheel of a car.

–JC

Dear God, You are the great giver of dreams, gifts and talents. Please show me by the power of Your Holy Spirit the area of service where I can bring the most glory to Your holy name. Thank You.

TODAY'S READING: EXODUS 31:1-6; 35:10; 36:1; MATTHEW 7:7-11;
PROVERBS 1; JEREMIAH 1:5

The Test

Put me on trial, LORD, and cross-examine me.
Test my motives and affections.

PSALM 26:2

By the time I was 16, I had been driving go-carts and winning races. I already had a pile of trophies, and I thought I was a big hotshot race-car driver. I knew how to drive, but I still had to take the test everyone else has to take if I wanted to get a driver's license. I easily passed the written test and was confident about the behind-the-wheel exam.

My examiner didn't like me much—I could tell from the get-go. In a race car, and on a go-cart particularly, the driver gasses with his right foot and brakes with his left foot. He drives with both feet.

I started off gassing and braking, gassing and braking. That upset my examiner. He asked me where I learned to drive. Being a smart aleck, I said, "I'm a race-car driver!" I probably never should have said that.

From that moment on, the examiner was looking for a way to flunk me. We were traveling down the street, and he said, "You see that parking space down there? When you get to it, stop, back in and park."

It was the old parallel-parking test. When we got to the spot, I put on the brakes and I stopped. I started to back up but he said, "Never mind. You can go."

"It's not a problem," I pleaded. "I can back up. I know how to park."

"That's OK," the examiner rebutted. "You'll have to come back and take your test another time. I told you to come to a complete stop, back up and park the car. You stopped, but you never looked in your rearview mirror. You just came to a stop and started to back up."

He probably was right, but it really irked me. I had flunked my behind-the-wheel driving test and had to wait several weeks before I could take it again. The next time I didn't get the same examiner and I passed. But I didn't tell him I was a race-car driver.

—*DW*

Peter had been following Jesus for a long time, but he too had to take a test.

Jesus had warned Peter: "Before the rooster crows, you will deny me three times."[1]

"No way," the disciple who had tried to walk on water defended himself. "I'm ready to die for you. Didn't I whack off that guy's ear?"[2]

It embarrassed Peter to think that the Lord had such little confidence in him. After all, he was a big cheese in the Messiah's outfit. Then it happened.[3]

Jesus had already been taken away and been found guilty. Peter was sitting alone in the courtyard when a girl approached him and said, "You were with Jesus, for both of you are from Galilee." Peter loudly denied the connection: "I don't know what you are talking about!"[4]

Later, out by the gate, another girl noticed him and said to those standing around, "This man was with Jesus—from Nazareth." Again, Peter distanced himself from Jesus, this time with an oath: "I don't even know the man."[5]

After a while the men who had been standing nearby came over to Peter and said, "We know you are one of his disciples, for we can tell by your Galilean accent." Peter began to curse and swear: "I don't even know the man." Immediately—just as Jesus had said—the cock crowed.[6]

Peter did not have time to comprehend what he had done for at that moment Jesus was being dragged outside. Their eyes met. Peter got a sinking feeling in the pit of his stomach and went away, crying bitterly.[7]

Satan wanted Peter to mess up. Peter did not look in the rearview mirror, so he failed the test.

One mess up if not confessed usually leads to another. If the second isn't confessed, a third will follow. I call it the sin cycle. It will bring us down if we try to ride it. To Peter's credit, he confessed his sin and got ready for the next test. It came on Pentecost. Peter preached and three thousand people accepted Jesus as Messiah.[8] Five thousand made the same commitment the second time he spoke.[9] Peter passed that test with flying colors and ended up spending the night in jail.[10]

–GC

Father God, I want to pass the tests You have for me. When I fail, make me mindful of my sin that I might come to You with it right away. Help me to learn from my mess ups and not repeat them. Amen.

TODAY'S READING: MATTHEW 18:22; 26:69-75; LUKE 22:31;
ACTS 2:37-41; 4:1-4; PSALM 26:1-7

Hard Work and Stink

I am the true vine, and my Father is the gardener. He cuts off every branch that doesn't produce fruit, and he prunes the branches that do bear fruit so they will produce even more.

J O H N   1 5 : 1 - 2

When I was dating Stevie, she had horses and asked me if I could ride. I told her, "Oh, yeah." I thought, *How hard can it be?* That was my first mistake.

We met at the stable and she queried, "Can you ride bareback?"

"Sure! That's not a problem."

I was thinking like a race-car driver: *If she can do it, I can do it.* I assumed that we would walk the horses, but she envisioned our romping through the fields and swimming across a river—without saddles! It was supposed to be like a scene out of some movie.

I did not start off too well. Because there is no stirrup, I could not mount the quarter horse. Stevie had to give me a leg up. That was embarrassing, but it gets worse. I got atop the steed, but I kept on going. I just slid on over and fell off on the other side.

On the second try, I got on. Still a little embarrassed, I just sat there while the horse rested with one rear leg cocked up as he stood on the other three. Suddenly the horse shifted his weight. He didn't take a step, he just switched feet—I fell off again in a big ol' heap.

In all of her wisdom, Stevie said, "Maybe this wasn't such a good idea after all."

I asked if I could try riding with a saddle. That worked pretty well. But we didn't romp across the fields, and we definitely didn't swim the horses. I would have drowned. We just took a nice leisurely walk.

I gave horseback riding my best shot, but I stunk it up. Sometimes when you give it your best shot, you still fall off the horse.

–DW

What happens if we put an unwrapped onion in the refrigerator? It makes everything else stinky. Get down on the kitchen floor and open the refrigerator door. What comes wafting out? Onion smell. P.U.! Why do onions stink? It is what onions do.

God has made it clear: There will be no stink in heaven. God is perfectly holy, and He will not spend eternity in the presence of stink. That's a big problem for us because we all have a sin nature. We've all sinned, and sin makes us stink. Basically, we're all onions. God won't let anyone stink up high heaven.

How do we solve the problem? Cooking an onion reduces the stink, but it doesn't eliminate the odor. Life is a pressure cooker that definitely cuts down on stench, but cooked onions still stink up a refrigerator. Regardless of the degree, because we reek, God is left with either throwing us away or wrapping us in Cling Wrap. The latter is the blood of Christ. It's our covering.

Some theologians argue that as new creatures in Christ we no longer have a sin nature, and once we have received Christ we spend the rest of our lives trying to break old habit patterns. Maybe, but Paul had a problem.[1] Whether we call it sin nature or our flesh, it stunk.

How hard would the onion have to work to stop stinking? It is a foolish question. An onion's odor is one of its properties. The solution is the Handi-wrap of Jesus. God wraps us up in Christ and plants a seed in our center. The seed sprouts, and we become something new. It may take a while to shed the old covering, but it is something God will do if we let Him.

In Jesus we aren't an onion anymore, but apart from Him we stink—and not even our best shot will solve that problem.

–*JC*

Dear Lord of heaven and Earth, thank You for covering my sin through the death of Your Son. I confess that I let my old nature get the better of me sometimes. But I want victory over my old ways, so cook me that I might look more like Jesus. Then empower me with Your Holy Spirit and help me to make decisions that will be pleasing in Your sight. Amen.

TODAY'S READING: JOHN 15:1-11; ROMANS 7:7-25; 8:1-11; GALATIANS 5:16-24

Running from God

Be careful! Watch out for attacks from the Devil, your great enemy. He prowls around like a roaring lion, looking for some victim to devour.

1 PETER 5:8

Put on all of God's armor so that you will be able to stand firm against all strategies and tricks of the Devil. For we are not fighting against people made of flesh and blood, but against the evil rulers and authorities of the unseen world, against those mighty powers of darkness who rule this world, and against wicked spirits in the heavenly realms.

EPHESIANS 6:11-12

A friend had a brand-new 1969 GTO with three deuces. It was a four-speed and fast. He got it for his birthday, but he didn't know how to drive it. We had been drinking and everybody was a little loose. We wanted to see what the car could do, so I put it through the paces. Someone had a not-so-bright idea: "Hey, DW, I hear you are pretty good at outrunnin' the cops. Let's get 'em to chase us. That'd be fun!"

Just as I was telling my friends no way, a police officer pulled up beside us. One of the guys in the backseat of the GTO flipped a beer can over our car, and it landed on the cop's hood. With that, the race was on. For the next several hours, every police car in Owensboro, Kentucky, was, at one time or another, involved. That's close to 30 cars. Six of them wrecked during the chase. It was just like *Smokey and the Bandit.*

Whenever I saw a roadblock, I would throw the GTO sideways and take off down another side street. We finally made it out of town, and we were all laughing, thinking this was the coolest thing we had ever done. I pulled the GTO into a driveway, went up a hill and turned around. About then a police car turned into the driveway, and the cop saw us. We were blocked, nose-to-nose.

I backed up a bit and he pulled up a bit. I was not about to give up, so I warned my friends: "OK, here we go, boys." I backed up the GTO, stopped real fast and then tore out through the yard. The police officer stood up and started shooting. Bam! Bam! Bam! Bam! Bam! Bam!

Everybody in the GTO screamed. "You bunch of wimps," I said, shushing them. "You believe he's gonna shoot real bullets at us? He's shootin' blanks. He isn't gonna shoot us for outrunnin' the cops."

We got away once again, but by this time we were running low on gas. We stopped at a little country store and while we pumped fuel, we spotted six huge holes down the side of the GTO. Six holes! The cop hadn't been shooting at the tires!

I thought he had just been playing, but he had been playing for real.

After we got gas, we drove around the county and came back through the other side of town. My friend, who owned the GTO, was worried and asked, "What am I gonna do?"

I was working at a garage at the time and it had a body shop. I assured everyone: "We'll have it fixed tomorrow. We'll bondo those holes and paint it. Then the cops will say, 'It can't be the same car. It doesn't have any holes in it.'"

The next afternoon, we got another not-so-bright idea: We decided to go see what the car looked like in daylight. When we got to the body shop, the police surrounded us and we got busted.

–DW

<hr>

In this *Smokey-and-the-Bandit* chase the cops were the good guys, and DW was out sinning on a limb. How did it turn out? DW will reveal that in the next reading. But the story up to this point reminds me of another chase that goes on every day. While it is not an exact parallel, how often do we try to outrun God?

We get together with our friends and party away. It feels good, and we experience a rush. Before we know it, we do something we know we should not, but by then the chase is on. We go down every side street we can find and cut across every field, dodging God. When we come face-to-face with Him, we take two steps back and, rather than face our sin, we flee again. We assure everyone that He understands our need for a thrill. We even unwittingly fool ourselves into believing that our sin will only shoot out our tires, at worst.

When we flee God, it is only when we run out of gas that we see that our sin has done more damage than we thought. Still, too often, we do not stop to ask, Is the thrill worth it?   *–JC*

Lord God of all authority and power, don't let the enemy sift and devour me or the ones I love. Keep us from temptation; deliver us from evil. You can do it because all power, glory and honor are Yours. Thank You.

TODAY'S READING: 1 PETER 5:7-11; JAMES 4:7-8;
EPHESIANS 6:10-20; LUKE 22:31-34

Two Guys in One

What this means is that those who become Christians become new persons. They are not the same anymore, for the old life is gone. A new life has begun!

2 CORINTHIANS 5:17

The wild ride was over in an instant. My friends and I had outrun the cops the night before, but they had caught up with us. Even though I had been driving, they arrested the owner of the car who had been riding shotgun. The cop who had shot at us remembered his face and assumed he had been driving.

The guy was more of an acquaintance—he wasn't a part of our main group of friends—and his dad had money, so we decided that since the cops thought he had been driving, we would not tell the truth. We all agreed to let him take the fall.

The whole mess ended up in court. The prosecutor suggested I take the Fifth Amendment. I didn't know what the Fifth Amendment was or why I needed to take it, but I agreed. I thought my friends and I had a deal and I was safe. In court, I had a surprise coming. The prosecuting attorney announced, "These four guys are trying to frame Waltrip, because Waltrip doesn't have anything to lose. Waltrip doesn't have a driver's license and he doesn't have any insurance."

My mind was buzzing: *What? That ain't the way this is supposed to go.* My friends were all scooting away from me. They were telling the truth; but because the officer who shot the car mistakenly said the owner had been driving, they found him guilty. He paid a huge fine.

I didn't say anything—and I got off—but not for free. I lost three friends. It would have been cheaper to have paid the fine. I never made up with my buddies before we went our separate ways. And strangely enough, I never saw the owner of the car again. I don't know where he went or what happened to him. It was like he fell off the face of the earth.

If you party, you'll always pay in some way. We all lost something as a result of our "good time," and we could have lost our lives. I am glad I survived long enough to let God get a hold of me.

–DW

When Darrell speaks in public he often starts by saying, "My wife says she's been married to two men with the same name. There is the me before I was saved, and the new me after I was saved."

It boggles my mind that a Vanderbilt woman would fall for a rowdy race-car driver and then do whatever it took to hold the marriage together until God changed him. DW was definitely out of control—outrunning cops, getting shot at, drinking. No wonder Stevie's dad, a Harvard grad, went to extreme measures to try to keep them from getting married.

DW reminds me of another guy who was two different guys. He reminds me of Saul, aka Paul. We know about his Damascus Road experience, but less is said about the changes that occurred in the man. This is the guy who held Stephen's coat while he was being stoned to death and whose claim to fame was the number of Christians he had killed before the Damascus Road encounter.[1]

After a blinding light dropped him and after Jesus had a little chat with him, it was the end of Saul and the beginning of Paul. He stopped killing Christians and started building the Church. In Paul's spare time, God had him write a big hunk of the New Testament. Paul even thought it was a privilege to suffer for the cause of Christ. He was lashed on five separate occasions; was beaten with rods three times; was stoned once; was shipwrecked three times; was adrift in the seas for a day and a night; and suffered through numerous other dangers, weariness, pain and sleepless nights. He even endured hunger and thirst.[2] He could handle all that because he had become a new creature in Christ.

I am two people with the same name, too. College friends remember me for my former vocabulary and my ability to hold the attention of a group of guys for as long as three hours with dirty joke after dirty joke. "What do you do now, Jay?" they ask.

"I'm a travelin' preacher."

"You're a what?"

"Yeah, I'm two people with the same name, and the old guy is dead."

Are you two different people with the same name? What are you going to do about it?

–*JC*

Oh great God of wonder, thank You for putting Your hand on me and changing me into something You can use to accomplish eternal results. Make me a new person in Christ. Amen.

TODAY'S READING: 2 CORINTHIANS 11:16-31;
1 CORINTHIANS 5:11-19; GALATIANS 6:11-16

Humble Pie

He leads the humble in what is right, teaching them his way.

PSALM 25:9

I was a rookie who didn't know diddly-squat, but there I was in my first Winston Cup race and I was up front with the leaders. I was passing cars left and right and keeping pace with drivers who usually won races. It was almost surreal, and I was sure that I was doing something wrong.

My crew chief was notorious for cheating. He would do things such as remove the restrictor plate to make the engine run better. I thought, *He must have done something. We must be cheatin' big-time!*

I had had to buy equipment before the race. I'd spent about $600 for a jack and air wrenches, and I had a ragtag pit crew. They had never in their lives done a choreographed four-tire change with air guns. They were one-at-a-time-with-a-lug-wrench guys.

I was feeling good when I came down pit road to take on four tires. In those days, the low 20-second range was good for a pit stop. It took my team about a minute.

When my car came down from the jack, I took off, but everyone was pointing at me. I thought, *Oh, no, they must know I'm cheatin'. Man, what am I gonna do?*

I had no idea that the jack was stuck on the jack stob under the side of the car. The stob sticks down and that's where you put the jack to raise the car. The crew hadn't let the jack all the way down—just far enough to get the wheels on the ground, so the jack was just dangling along beside the car.

I was going down pit road 120 miles an hour with a jack trailing along beside of me. When I finally built up enough speed, the jack flew out from under the car, hit a wall and busted into a million pieces.

It turns out I wasn't cheating. My car was just really fast. I would have won that race if I'd handled my pit crew properly. I beat myself and lost by a jack. What a way to learn a lesson on humility!

—DW

There are lessons to be learned by eating humble pie. I got a good one late one night a few years ago. My family and I had left the cat's litter box in the pantry one morning. Everyone else returned home before I did. Someone put the cat box in the garage, but not where it belonged. It was midnight when I arrived. My hands were full, so I didn't bother to turn on the light after I got out of the car. There was no reason; I knew the way.

I didn't step in the litter box, but neither did I step over it. I stepped on the side, creating a lever, turning the box into a medieval catapult. Cat stuff was thrown on the back of my legs and up into the air, with much of it coming down on my head, shoulders and in and on my shoes. A push of the light switch revealed the result: litter box contents were everywhere.

My wife and kids were at the back door by the time I got to it. They looked at me and observed the scene—then it registered. I was mad and it showed, so they tried not to smile or laugh. But there was no holding back. Someone snickered and that was that. They fell out guffawing. I couldn't help but join them. I beat myself because I didn't turn on the light, and I ate humble pie.

Humility doesn't come naturally. It has to be learned. It is an inward quality that helps us to not regard ourselves more highly than we should.[1] It is the way we are supposed to come to God[2] and how we are supposed to approach others.[3] It is an essential ingredient in salvation[4] and learning God's ways.[5]

I have to admit that I actually enjoyed the litter-box lesson in humility. It was a very good laugh. I suppose I could have played the macho dad and ranted and raved, but the picture of me standing there with cat stuff in my hair and on my shoulders was just too funny. I'm glad I didn't miss the moment, as humbling as it was.

–GC

Father, I hesitate to ask that You humble me under Your mighty hand, because the unknown is a really scary place and I don't know how hard the lesson will be; but I will trust You with the outcome. Amen.

TODAY'S READING: ROMANS 12:3–13:7; JAMES 1:19-22;
MATTHEW 18:1-6; PSALM 25:9

The Other Hand

Don't copy the behavior and customs of this world, but let God transform you into a new person by changing the way you think. Then you will know what God wants you to do, and you will know how good and pleasing and perfect his will really is.

ROMANS 12:2

On the racetrack, everything happens at 180 miles an hour. We go the length of a football field in about a second. To survive, we need quick reflexes and good instincts. When we're going along and cars are wrecking, we can't pause and ponder, *Hmm, I think I'll go low* or *Maybe I'll do such and such* or *I guess I'll just do this or that*. At that speed there is no time to think.

Good drivers instinctively react instantly. The ones who aren't so good do not process the big picture fast enough. We know who the slow thinkers are and we avoid them.

Each track has its own quirks and idiosyncrasies. The more a racer drives each one, the better equipped he is to go back. Talladega is easy to drive. Anyone can go 210 miles per hour at Talladega, if he is on the track by himself. The problem arises when there are 43 cars all hanging together, three and four wide. Since all racers know how to drive fast, we don't string out. Being that close to so many cars for 500 miles mentally exhausts a person. And when someone wrecks, it wrecks a lot of cars.

Dover is a one-mile track, banked 24 degrees in the corners and 9 degrees in the straights. We call it self-cleaning because when someone hits the wall, his car slides down to the inside of the track. At Dover, we know that if there is trouble ahead, we need to stay high. Bristol is a half-mile lap. It is the most physically demanding track because of its 32-degree banked turns.

Darlington is called the Lady in Black and is the oldest superspeedway. It was built 45 or so years ago and was designed for cars to run on it at 120 miles per hour. We race on it today at over 180 miles per hour.

Charlotte is everybody's favorite racetrack because a lot of drivers are based in North Carolina and it feels like home.

–DW

In the world, much of life happens at warp speed. The driver on the highway cuts us off. How will we react? The double-scoop mint-chip ice-cream cone looks so tempting. Should we enjoy it? The job offer comes in, but we must decide whether to take it. Should we say yes? Each day, we must make a zillion small and large decisions. To survive we cannot freeze; rather, we need to instinctively react, and sometimes instantly.

To make right choices, we must draw upon the right source. Let me illustrate: I'm right-handed, so my left, or off hand, represents my flesh, my natural man—one possible source. My right hand represents the new creature that I became when I came to Jesus—another possible source.

When playing catch, I throw with my right hand, but I catch with my left. That's my natural way. I have to concentrate to make myself catch with my right hand. Likewise, when I have time to think, I usually respond as Christ would respond. But when something surprises me, my fleshly, sin-marred reflexes still dominate.

A guy once bit me on the wrist during a church-league basketball game, and I yelled, "What kind of [bleep] is this." More than six hundred church people heard my bleep. It was an embarrassing off-handed response. On the other hand, I have a friend who, while rock climbing, broke loose from the face of the rock and fell. He had six feet to fall in the air before he would find out if his safety rope would hold. If it did, he would bounce a bit but be alive. If it broke, he would die. As his fall began, he yelled, "God help me!"

I reacted with my off hand. My friend reacted with his right hand. I find that the more I reach across with my off hand, the less my right hand responds. Conversely, the more I allow my right hand to flex, the less my off hand reaches across. To achieve the godly response, we must discipline our natural reflexes by reinforcing Christlike behavior. When we act like Christ, we will find ourselves instantly reacting instinctively with our right hand—even when someone bites us on the left.

—*GC*

God of heaven, I want to be more and more pleasing in Your sight. I want to overcome the old ways. Remind me to practice doing what Jesus would do so that I might get better at reacting the way He would react. Amen.

TODAY'S READING: PSALM 48:10; ROMANS 12:1-2; MATTHEW 12:33-37; PHILIPPIANS 2:5-8; COLOSSIANS 3:16-17

The Checkered Flag

*I have fought a good fight, I have finished the race,
and I have remained faithful.*

2 TIMOTHY 4:7

In racing, we have several flags. Green means go. It is used at the start of the race and to restart a race after a yellow or red flag.

Yellow means caution. A wreck, debris or anything else wrong on the track that could impact the racers will bring it out. When there is trouble, we have to slow down and hold our positions. If we change spots, we'll get a black flag, which means that we have violated a rule.

We have to periodically stop for gas and tires. If we have to stop when the race is going full tilt, we'll lose more positions than if the cars are slowed down due to a caution flag. We can go into the pits if there is a yellow flag. Also, when a yellow flag is out, the cars close ranks. This gives drivers an opportunity to pass the car ahead when the green flag comes out. If we need to get into the pits or want to pass another car, sometimes we will hope for a yellow flag.

Red means stop. Regardless of where we are on the track, we have to stop. Big wrecks will bring out the red flag.

White means it is the last lap. If the competition is close, this is where the most intense racing occurs.

A checkered flag means the race is over. When you cross the line under the checkered flag, your position is set. If you started the race and didn't finish, all those who did finish are positioned ahead of you. But every position is awarded points.

Lights around the track represent these flags. When an official waves a flag, the corresponding lights come on so that all of the racers simultaneously know which flag has been waved. If the black flag is out, a number corresponding to the car being flagged is illuminated and that car must go into the pits. If a severe violation has occurred, the car is disqualified. If it's a lesser infraction, the car may be sent to the rear of the field or may be penalized a certain number of laps.

–DW

Jesus told us to make disciples of all people, baptize them and teach them to obey God.[1] That's what we are supposed to be doing when the green flag is out. However, in our race we aren't competing against other racers. We are competing against ourselves and against the enemy of our souls who wants to wreck us.

Sometimes we have to slow down. God wants us to come into the pits at least every seven days to gather with other believers.[2] There are times when He wants us to get away to pray and fast. Often we have to slow down to help fellow racers who have had trouble or wrecked on the track. As believers, we want to close ranks and help as many people finish as we can.

Sometimes we get stopped, and it's no fault of our own. There are times when our kids or friends spin out and take us with them. Circumstances can bump us from behind and send us into the wall. Getting stopped is part of life. What's important is to get going again when the green flag comes back out.

In the Christian race, the white flag is for those nearing the end. It comes out for younger people who are terminally ill, but most people see the white flag during their nursing-home years or the equivalent.

The black flag is for the people who get disqualified, like the unrepentant sinners, posers and pretenders whom Jesus talked about.[3] He said there are some who tenderly call Him Lord, but they don't really mean it. On that day when others are getting a checkered flag, they'll get a black one.

The checkered flag is waved when we meet the Lord face-to-face. It's great to finish well, but it's crucial at least to finish. Leg it if you have to. Just finish. Stumblers, bumblers, fumblers and former backsliders can all cross the finish line. The ideal is to hear God say, "Well done, my good and faithful servant."[4]

–GC

Gracious Lord, I want to give my all in the running of this race. Help me to fulfill the calling You have given me and let me do it for Your glory, not mine. When I get the checkered flag, I long to hear "Well done." May it be so.

TODAY'S READING: 2 TIMOTHY 4:7-8; EPHESIANS 2:4-6; 2 TIMOTHY 2:15

Bad to the Bone

Now the sons of Eli were scoundrels who had no respect for the LORD.

1 SAMUEL 2:12

We were at a track in Indianapolis. I was the gunslinger who had just ridden into town. I set a track record, I won the heat race, and I won the trophy dash. Everybody was asking, "Hey, who is this guy?" I was competing against two brothers who race there all the time. I could only guess about their upbringing, but they appeared to fit the mean Mafia stereotype.

Next up was the feature race. These brothers wanted to make sure I didn't win it. These two cats were side by side, holding me back, working together to lock me in. I came off the corner, and they left a little room. I was about to make my move. They realized what I was going to do—I was going to try to close up the hole, forcing them to slam into each other and wreck. One knocked a hole in the wall, and the race was stopped so that the wall could be fixed.

I was sitting in my car behind the pace car when I saw a guy coming down the racetrack with a jack handle. He started pounding my race car and tried to beat me. I had a window net. Without it, he might have killed me. He bashed my car into pieces before they apprehended him. Stevie and her sister were in the grandstand, and Stevie's sister asked what was going on. Stevie said, "I don't know. I think they're putting a wedge in it." That was the only term she knew at that time, and it's what we do to make adjustments during a race. However, the man with the jack handle was not trying to fix my car, he was trying to put a wedge in me.

The promoter rushed out to my car. He told me not to win the race or the two guys would kill him, and he was serious. I could have won, but I chose to finish second.

At the end of the race, the officials stopped my car on the back straightaway, surrounded it with police cars, brought in my hauler and loaded my race car. They made Stevie, her sister and me lie down in the backseat of a police car as they escorted us out of there. Those two Mafia-type dudes were dangerous.

Stevie's sister could hardly believe any of this: "And you do this for a livin'?"

−DW

If DW had been racing in Samuel's day, he might have run into Eli's boys. They were mean Mafia types, too.

Eli had two sons, Hophni and Phinehas. The brothers were bad to the bone. They were the equivalent of organized crime at the time. One of their favorite exploits was to steal part of the sacrifices the people brought to God, which actually was stealing from God Himself. But that was not the end of it. They got rich selling sacrificed food, and they grew fat when they ate too much of what they couldn't sell. Plus, they seduced young women who served in the temple area. They had problems with the big three: money, sex and power. What's new?

Hophni and Phinehas were Levites and were in charge of worship, but treating the Lord's offerings with contempt made it extra bad. "The sin of these young men was very serious in the Lord's sight."[1]

Eli had overlooked the boys' atrocities for years, but when he was old, more complaints came in than could be swept under the rug. Eli gave his sons a scolding and asked them to shape up, but he didn't make them behave. Eli had lost control of his sons many years before. He was your classic soft, permissive parent who didn't have the heart to be firm when they were young and didn't have the clout when he was old.

God spoke to Eli, "So why do you scorn my sacrifices and offerings? Why do you honor your sons more than me?"[2] Then God cursed Eli's family, and Hophni and Phinehas died on the same day.[3]

The Pharisees were the Mafia types of Jesus' day. Like Eli's boys, pretending to be pious, they used religion for power to bully and intimidate. They too were bad to the bone. Jesus let them know what he thought about their behavior. When the Son of God says "Woe to you" eight times in a row, it ought to get your attention.[4] It didn't, but it should have. Hell would be their reward.

We do not know what happened to those brothers who wanted to kill DW. We just know that they were mean dudes and that God is a God of justice—which is the last thing you want from God if you are mean. Hophni, Phinehas and the Pharisees found that out the hard way.

–JC

Heavenly Father, forgive me for the times when I have been a bully and misused my power and position. Forgive me when I have the wrong attitude toward children, the poor, widows, the sick and afflicted, and others who are weak. Help me to demonstrate the love of Jesus Christ to those without power.

TODAY'S READING: 1 SAMUEL 1:9-28; 2:11-17,22-34; 8:1-3;
MATTHEW 23:13-29; EPHESIANS 6:3

Car Number 490

Then Peter came to him and asked, "Lord, how often should
I forgive someone who sins against me? Seven times?"
"No!" Jesus replied, "seventy times seven!"

MATTHEW 18:21-22

In racing, each car has a designated number. Low numbers are considered the more important ones. Having a low number means that a driver has been around a while.

To get a number, a driver has to call NASCAR and tell them that he is entering competition and to let them know which car or cars he'll be racing that year. NASCAR will give him a list of available numbers, and he can pick one.

Early in my career, I had been number 48 on the short tracks. When I started racing in the Winston Cup series in 1972, I was hoping to initially get the same digits, but James Hilton was 48. NASCAR gave me 95. I've also been 88 and 11, but I always really wanted 17, because that was David Pearson's number and he had been my childhood hero.

After a year or two, Pearson retired and the number 17 became available. My crew chief at the time, Jake Elder, had been the crew chief on Pearson's car, and he wanted 17, too. He said, "Long as we got that 95 number, we're never gonna win. We've got to have a low number to win races." That's old-school thinking, but it was OK with me.

We got number 17 and I became very attached to it. I won the Daytona 500 on my 17th try. The race was on the 17th day of the month. I was in pit stall number 17 and the purse was $1.7 million. My golf handicap is 17. My home is built on lot number 17. My daughter, Jessica Lee, was born on the 17th. My name "Darrell Lee Waltrip" has 17 letters in it. Seventeens everywhere! It is obvious why it's my favorite number.

When I retired, I gave 17 to Matt Kenseth, and he's running it now. Matt won the Winston Cup Championship in 2003 with my number. I still like number 17, but nowadays the number 7 is growing on me, too.

—DW

Seven seems to be one of God's favorite numbers. It occurs 391 times in the King James version of the Bible. The number 12 shows up 165 times and the number 40 is in there 145 times. I don't know all of the reasons why, but clearly seven is a biggie.

Seven symbolized God's perfection. Creation took seven days and God rested on the seventh day.[1] The people were to leave the ground fallow in the seventh year.[2] Major festivals were to be held on the last seven days of whatever was appropriate.[3] Pharaoh's dream had seven good years and seven bad ones.[4] Jacob worked two cycles of seven years.[5] The book of Revelation notes seven churches.[6]

Culturally, the process for making an oath was closely related to the number seven. A person would have to declare something seven times or bind oneself by seven statements. That's why Peter asked about forgiving a person seven times.[7]

God apparently likes multiples of seven, too. The year of Jubilee came every 49 years.[8] That's when all Jewish bond slaves were released and land reverted to its former owner. Another multiple of seven used in the Bible is 70. It is found 60 times. The Bible refers to 70 elders.[9] Seventy years is specified as the length of the exile.[10] And the messianic kingdom was to be inaugurated after a period of 70 weeks had passed.[11]

Jesus sent out the 70,[12] and He commanded that we forgive not just seven times, but 70 times seven—which really means do not count, just forgive however many times it takes.[13]

In high school I was number 55. As a player at Oregon State I wore number 20. When I was a Laker, I was number 52. If I drove in NASCAR, I would roll with 55. It is still my favorite. If God had a number on His car, it would probably be 7. But I like to think we should all be driving car 490, which is 70 times 7! Not only would it remind us to forgive, but it would also remind us of how completely we have been forgiven.

–GC

Tender, forgiving and merciful Father God, thank You for putting my sin as far away as the east is from the west. Thank You for totally and completely forgiving me 70 times 7 times. Help me to live my life out of gratitude for what You have done. Amen.

TODAY'S READING: LUKE 17:3-4; MATTHEW 18:21-35;
PSALM 103:8-14; COLOSSIANS 3:12-17

The Lone Ranger

*But God showed his great love for us by sending Christ to
die for us while we were still sinners.*

ROMANS 5:8

Race-car drivers are a bit like the Lone Ranger. He had his one-of-a-kind horse, Silver. Race-car drivers have cars with a one-of-a-kind paint job. Silver would rear up on his back legs at the end of the show when the Lone Ranger had beaten all of the bad guys. After a win, drivers like to show off for fans by doing a bunch of doughnuts or just smoking their tires. When a burnout is done right, the rear tires will blow. It's called "scorchin' the hides."

The Lone Ranger had a hat and a mask. Drivers have a triple-layered Nomex, fire-resistant suit. They also have gloves and a full-face helmet. In a fire, this equipment protects the drivers for 30 to 45 seconds.

Tonto was the Lone Ranger's faithful friend. Race-car drivers have their crew chiefs and crews. Drivers are allowed to have seven people over the wall when the car comes into the pits, and they cannot win unless the crew is good.

Silver bullets were the Lone Ranger's trademark. Being quick in the pits is ours. We can pump 11 gallons of gas into a car in 5.5 seconds, or we can add 22 gallons of fuel and change 4 tires in about 13.5 seconds.

The Lone Ranger knew how to take the heat. People always wanted to know who that masked man was. Drivers have to take the heat, too. It's 140 degrees in the race car—it is literally possible to fry an egg on the floorboard. Drivers have to wear protective boots on the back of their shoes to keep from cooking their heels. They also have a box bolted down on the right side of the car that takes in air through a scoop, makes it cold, removes carbon monoxide and blows the filtered air into the helmet.

The Lone Ranger was a mysterious man on a mission. Drop the green flag and drivers are on a serious mission, too. The Lone Ranger was invincible because he was the Lone Ranger. That's where the analogy ends because drivers only think they are.

—DW

Actor Clayton Moore portrayed the Lone Ranger and Fran Striker wrote "The Lone Ranger Creed." Here are a few of the points in that Creed: "[1] I believe that to have a friend, a man must be one. . . . [2] That God put the firewood there, but every man must gather and light it himself. . . . [3] That men should live by the rule of what is best for the greatest number. [4] That sooner or later, somewhere, somehow, we must settle with the world and make payment for what we have taken. [5] That all things change but truth, and that truth alone lives on forever."[1]

As I read the Creed, I wondered if it would stand up to biblical standards. The masked man got three out of five right.

The Lone Ranger must have been a good friend. Tonto stuck with him through thick and thin, and they were closer than brothers. Scripture often brings forth this concept, so that works.[2] True.

The "firewood" thought passes the biblical test as well. God gives us responsibility. If a man won't work, don't let him eat.[3] The disabled and others who cannot work are obvious exceptions. True.

Living by the rule of doing what is best for the greatest number of people does not cut it. If we live that way, we will ultimately make compromises against the weakest in society. Such compromise leads to abortion and euthanasia. Moreover, when the Lone Ranger roamed the West, society held to biblical values. Today much of that moral fiber has been chipped away. False.

Kimo Sabe (that's what Tonto called the Lone Ranger) almost got the "settling up" point right. But we don't settle with the world. We settle with the Father. The Lone Ranger had the correct debtor, but the wrong creditor. False.

There is no question about the masked man's last thought. He got it right. Way to go, Ranger! God's truth doesn't change.[4] True.

Did you ever notice that the masked man never stuck around? He learned that doing too much good can get a person killed. Jesus knew that risk. He discovered firsthand that when we try to give people what's best rather than what they want, they'll kill us. The Lone Ranger had to keep moving to save his skin. But Jesus stuck around because He wasn't concerned about His. He was concerned about ours.

–JC

Almighty God, thank You for good friends and for absolute truth. Give me the desire to do the work You have planned for me. I give You thanks for the joy of my salvation in Jesus Christ my Lord. Amen.

TODAY'S READING: PROVERBS 18:24; 2 THESSALONIANS 3:10; EXODUS 31:18–32:20; JUDGES 17:6; 2 JOHN 1:1-3; ROMANS 5:6-11

Riding on Rails

*So humble yourselves under the mighty power of God,
and in his good time he will honor you.*

1 PETER 5:6

The Lone Ranger was no better than his horse, Silver. If Silver had laid down on him on the way to save the day, the Lone Ranger would have been just another cowboy. It's the same way with a race car and its driver. A driver is no better than his car. It is like a marriage. If it's a good marriage, the driver gets good performance out of the car. If it's a bad marriage, he gets weak performance or wrecks.

In a turn, when a car is too loose, the rear tires lose traction before the front tires do, the car oversteers, and the rear end wants to come around, causing the car to spin. When a car is too tight, the front tires lose traction before the rear tires do, the car understeers, and it wants to head for the wall. When the car is balanced, it goes around the track like it's on rails. A person becomes the driver in the fullest sense of the word when the car is balanced.

The racer can be either the driver or just a passenger who just happens to be sitting behind the steering wheel. When he is in control, the car is balanced—he can put it where he wants, when he wants. When the racer is the driver and not a passenger, he can concentrate on the driving and not worry about where the car is going to go.

The racer is merely a passenger when the car is too loose or too tight: It takes him where it wants to go, and he is constantly trying to keep it from going where he does not want it to go. On the track, we call this "hanging onto it."

A racer can't drive smart when he is a passenger who is just hanging on. The car will beat him. A great driver has to be in control; and for the driver to be in control, the car has to be balanced. A driver can only be at his best when he is riding on rails.

—DW

Let's call the car our sin nature. When it's loose or tight, we're a passenger and it's in control. We're in control when we balance the natural with the supernatural things of God. We're driving when God is in control, but we're a passenger when our sin nature is in control.

Samuel of the Old Testament was driving when he arrived at Jesse's house to anoint a king. Samuel knew the moment he saw David that he was the chosen one. God told him. We can hear God's voice when He's in control. As passengers we either won't be listening or there will be too much other noise to hear God.

In David's case, God took an obscure driver, put him in His best car and gave him the best team. As long as David kept his car balanced, he did really well. Even during times of testing, waiting and running for his life, David drove like he was riding on rails.

After David became king, the first time he didn't fulfill his responsibilities the car got loose. His sin nature took over. He pulled a peeping David and hit the wall with the neighbor lady, Bathsheba. Then he hit it again when he had her husband killed to cover up the fact that he had impregnated her. That's what happens when you get out of balance. You wreck.

David lived with his sin for about two years. Then God used Nathan to get in his face and David turned around by writing the greatest words of repentance ever penned—Psalm 51. He balanced the car.

Sin grieves and quenches the Spirit of God. When that happens, we can't hear God until we repent. Repentance puts our car back in balance.

We may not have done biggie sins like David, but at one time or another we have each allowed our car to get loose. We have all sinned.

Take control of the sin nature by putting God back in control of your life. Pray Psalm 51 and you'll soon be riding on rails.

–*GC*

Create in me a clean heart, O God. Renew a right spirit within me. Do not banish me from Your presence, and don't take Your Holy Spirit from me. Restore to me again the joy of Your salvation, and make me willing to obey You. Then I will teach Your ways to sinners, and they will return to You.[1] Amen.

TODAY'S READING: PSALM 51; 1 PETER 5:6-11

The Eye of the Storm

*The wise are cautious and avoid danger; fools plunge
ahead with great confidence.*

PROVERBS 14:16

My philosophy was *Don't race against people who can't beat you.* On the track, I would always avoid putting myself into a situation in which there would be a bunch of guys around me who could not keep up. If I let that happen, I would beat myself by messing with those drivers. It's kind of like getting in an argument with a fool.

Have you seen squirrels in the road? You don't know what they're going to do or where they're going to go. They might run under your tires or they might run away—you never know. The inexperienced drivers can be like squirrels. The young ones drive every lap like it's a qualifying lap. They can take you out in an instant. You want to get away from them. I would either go ahead or go behind. The more of them there are, the harder it is to get ahead. It's easier to just stay behind them.

Getting older and having kids made dropping back an easy decision, because I knew the young drivers would wreck. Besides, when you're older you no longer like wrecking. In fact, I didn't want to be up in the middle in what I call the eye of the storm. The eye of the storm is where all the squirrels are running around in circles—that's where the young drivers cluster and end up banging into each other.

I usually finished at Daytona and Talladega, and I finished pretty well, because I would not race against other drivers there. They usually have multicar crashes at those two tracks—sometimes up to 20 cars. My theory was *Even if I'm down two laps, it's better than being wrecked.* I was like a buzzard. I'd just fly around the racetrack and wait for the others to wreck. Then I'd come motoring on through. I might be a lap or two down, but I'd be in the top 20. And the top 20 was a whole lot better than being on the hood. I finished well in a number of Daytona and Talladega races and never raced against a soul. I just rode around and avoided the eye of the storm.

–DW

I'm still thinking about a summer camp experience from a few years ago. We showed a film about two girls who were on summer vacation. One planned on losing her virginity and did. The other wrestled with the decision to give herself to her boyfriend and didn't—with her dad's help. We followed the flick with a Q & A session.

One scene in the film showed a guy trying to seduce the virgin. The crowd consisted of primarily middle-class, white church kids who cheered for the guy to score. But during the interview time, the answers were what you would expect to hear in Sunday School.

Later that day, a man who had brought a small group of inner-city kids to camp approached me. He had a deeply concerned look on his face. I knew we needed to talk.

"My kids are used to doing wrong, and quite frankly, they still want to do wrong," he began. "They didn't know the difference between right and wrong for a long time. But even though they want to do wrong, they aren't, because they would rather be pleasing to God. Their talk isn't always right, but their actions have been."

This man's burden was heavy. He needed release from its weight. "What's your point?" I prodded.

"It seems like most of the kids in that room were saying the right things but are doing the wrong things. They've got the talk down pat, but I don't see the actions to back it up. I think those church kids are a bad influence on my kids." That leader was smart enough to see the eye of the storm and get out of it before it caused a wreck.

The eye of the storm can occur anyplace at any time, even at church or summer camp. We will find plenty of people who are sold out to Christ in both places, but we cannot assume all are. Casual Christians are like squirrels. You can't depend on them. Those who call themselves believers but aren't committed to Christ can wreck in a heartbeat. If a person's walk doesn't match his or her talk, take a lesson from DW and that inner-city youth leader and get away. Stay out of the eye of the storm.

–*GC*

Loving protector, show me when I am moving into the eye of a storm.
Direct me to those to whom I should minister, but give me the courage to
walk away from those who would hurt my relationship with You. Please
show me when I need to stand and when I need to run. Thank You.

TODAY'S READING: PROVERBS 1:10-19; 3:5-7; 4:14-19,27; 14:16; 16:17;
MATTHEW 21:28-32; 1 THESSALONIANS 5:21-22

Turning Over Tables

First pride, then the crash—the bigger the ego, the harder the fall.

PROVERBS 16:18, *THE MESSAGE*

Success went straight to my head. I was the Muhammad Ali of NASCAR. I was obnoxious. I would make predictions about what I was going do, and then I'd go out and do it. It was part of the game.

Stevie grew tired of my thinking that I was the most incredible human being who ever walked on Earth. Fans became irritated, too. Some even wore T-shirts that read "Anybody but Waltrip." Seems that people either loved me or hated me—there was no in-between.

At that time, I looked at racing differently. I thought it was a show and that I was a showman. This came naturally. I could be a showoff, and I could have a lot of fun when I was winning. At one point, I finished in the top five in 21 out of 28 races. When I had my mojo workin', I rode it.

God was very tolerant with me. I had a great run. I believe God allowed it to happen. And I also believe that when God said, "Okay, enough's enough," He took the success away. He's really patient, kind and diligent in waiting on us to come to Him. But if we don't come, sooner or later He will get our attention.

I won my last race in 1992. After that, it seemed that it didn't matter what I did. All the things I had done to achieve success, I couldn't seem to do anymore. Until then, I hadn't needed the best car or the best team because I was the best driver. Suddenly, I couldn't win or even drive by myself. I needed the best car and I needed the best team—everything had to go right. Of course, I never could get everything right. No one can. As a result, my life became harder and harder.

Our heart is where our treasure is, and my heart was in racing. God had to remove racing so that I could give my heart to Him. It took 10 years in the wilderness to get my heart right. But it took Moses 40 years, so I guess I got off easy.

—DW

It was the Passover. People were coming from everywhere to observe the occasion. Traveling long distances often made it difficult to bring a sacrifice. Others had currency they needed to exchange. Seeing the opportunity, some businessmen set up shop. There was money to be made. The chief priest controlled the enterprise and got a piece of the action.

The outer courts of the Temple had been sectioned off. Stalls, tables and merchandise filled the halls. Everyone was yelling and selling, like carnival hucksters. It was noisy and busy, just like the floor of a very old New York Stock Exchange.

Jesus came in to worship. A hush didn't come over the crowd. Nobody noticed. Nobody cared. There was money to be made and things to be bought.

Jesus seldom got angry, not even when He was mistreated, beaten and killed. However, He did get mad when God was affronted. I guess that is why He showed anger this time, or at least appeared to show it. The Bible does not actually use the word "anger," but we assume He was. Jesus made a scourge of cords and turned the tables on the vendors by turning over their tables.[1]

One man drove all of the vendors from the Temple. That didn't happen by His saying, "Okay fellas, you will have to quit making money and leave now." How could one man clean house in the Temple? Have you ever seen God mad? Me neither. But think about it. God was that man, and who was going to stand in His way? Nobody.

God wants His temple clean so that it is fit for worship. Worshiping is the first of the two commandments that summarize the law: We must love the Lord our God with everything we have got.[2] But we can't offer acceptable worship with a dirty temple.

If our heart isn't right, our temple is dirty. DW's heart wasn't right and God finally decided it was time to clean house. God had been patient for almost 10 years, and then He turned over the tables in DW's life. The choice is ours: Get out a broom and start sweeping, or watch God turn the tables.

–*JC*

Heavenly Father, I know Your Holy Spirit dwells in the temple that is my body. Show me if I am hiding dirt in secret places. I deeply desire to keep the temple clean. I want to confess my sin, and I repent of doing it again. I want a clean heart, O God. Forgive me and restore me. Amen.

TODAY'S READING: PROVERBS 16:18-19; JOHN 2:13-22; MATTHEW 22:36-40; PSALM 18:24-27

NASCAR people are wanderers. We go where the schedule tells us to go. During the season we arrive at a track on Wednesday or Thursday and leave after the race on Sunday. We go home for two or three days, and then we're off again. It's a crazy life.

In the 1980s, nobody in NASCAR had motor homes. Bringing one to the track wasn't the thing to do. Even if somebody had wanted to bring one, there was no place to park it, except in the infield with all the rowdy fans. Drivers need their rest before race day, so we stayed in hotels.

My daughter Jessica was born in 1987, just before we went to Florida for the Daytona 500. Stevie didn't want to sit in the back of the hauler with the baby, plus she wanted to be at the track.

I had seen entertainers around Nashville who had big motor homes. That gave me an idea. I went to a place in Nashville where entertainers lease their motor homes.

That is how it all started. We rented a coach, got a driver and took off for Florida. We even took my mom and dad with us. We parked the motor home in the most secure place we could, but there really wasn't an ideal location. We settled for where the members of the media parked their vehicles, so that the race fans wouldn't bother us.

After Daytona, we often leased a coach. We would use it at the track during the day; then go to the hotel at night. We would hire a babysitter for the race so that Stevie could keep laps. When other drivers saw what we were doing, they started doing it, too. After about three years of parking with the media, we asked NASCAR officials for a place for the competitors to park their motor homes.

Now, all of us wanderers can have our home with us as we go. The schedule still directs us, but at least we don't have to live in hotel rooms anymore.

–DW

DW wandered with the NASCAR community for more than 30 years as a driver. As a broadcaster, he's still wandering. The schedule of events still dictates where he will go.

Moses was a wanderer, too. When he led the Israelites out of Egypt, they became a community of wanderers. There was not a schedule or map to show them where to go; instead, they had a theophany. God appeared in physical form as a pillar of cloud by day and a pillar of fire by night. When the Jewish people were camped, the pillar of cloud would rest on the Tabernacle of God in the center of the Tent of Meeting. At night, it would change to a pillar of fire. The presence of the pillars assured the people that God was in their midst.

When the pillars moved so did the people. They broke camp as quickly as they could—even removing the bread from their ovens before it rose—and followed the pillar until it rested in another place. When the pillar stopped, the Jewish people stopped and made a new camp. Sometimes they stayed in the new place just one night—sometimes they stayed a few days or a few years. Not knowing when they would next be on the move kept them looking at the pillars.

These days God uses His Holy Word, His Holy Spirit and the counsel of other believers to guide us. Instead of watching two pillars, we read, pray and listen. However, the rule hasn't changed. God wants us to be constantly concentrating on Him, waiting for direction. He wants us restfully available and instantly obedient.

We don't know when He's going to move us and we don't know where we'll be going, but just like the wanderers of old, we must remain ready to move on a moments notice. There may be times when we'd like to move, but God will want us to stay put. Our job is to let God be in charge of the schedule.

—GC

Holy God, I love Your Word. Thank You for it. Thank You for hearing and answering my prayers. Speak loudly in my ear through the power of Your Spirit and Your people. I pledge to do whatever You say and to go wherever You tell me to go. Amen.

TODAY'S READING: EXODUS 13:17-22 (FOR THE STORY ON THE TWO PILLARS); NUMBERS 9:15-22; PHILIPPIANS 2:12-13; PSALM 16:7-8

The challenger. Driving car number 11 (above), DW often finished first and celebrated in Victory Lane (below).

The champion. DW jumped at every opportunity he had to take home another trophy. He celebrates after winning his fifth World 600 (left) and taking the checkereds in 1989 at the Atlanta International Speedway (below).

Fig Leaves

So, we are lying if we say we have fellowship with God but go on living in spiritual darkness. We are not living in the truth.

1 JOHN 1:6

We were at Dover and the car wasn't handling quite right. We decided to change a spring in the right front. That's hard to do during a race, but a caution flag came out which allowed us to go into the pits. We jacked up the car. It was possible to get the spring out, but it was going to take a while. We thought we could do it in 30 seconds and not lose a lap. Jeff Hammond, my crew chief, reached in and pulled out the spring, but he couldn't get the new one in. He was twisting and trying, but it would not go in.

We could not let the car down without the spring in there. And the pace car was close. The spotters hollered: "The pace car's comin' off turn four. You've gotta go, you've gotta go!" Finally, Hammond got the spring shoved in there. The crew dropped the car down off the jack, and I started to go, but they were hollering, "Whoa, whoa, whoa!" I thought they were saying, "Go, go, go!"

I flew down pit lane and as I got to the end, the hood flew up. It stayed hinged, but it slammed back against the top of the car so that I could not see what was ahead. I had to drive an entire lap looking out the side of the windshield. Then I stopped to try to get the hood closed. But the hood was all beat up and it wouldn't go down. We had people jumping up and down on it, trying to get it to shut so we could put the pins back in it.

Before the problem with the spring, we had been running in the top 10 or 15 and moving up in the pack. When the hood would not shut, we went from being a contender with a chance to have a decent finish to being laps down. We should have just left that spring alone. This was one of those times when we practiced one of Waltrip's Laws: *If it ain't broke, work on it until it is.*

–DW

I had an embarrassing moment in Fort Leavenworth, Kansas, during a chapel meeting. The place was full of officers in full dress and their wives. I had worked out late in the afternoon and polished off a 44-ounce Diet Pepsi too close to speaking time. I was winding up my message and had to visit the restroom something fierce.

The chaplain was going to close in prayer, so I wrapped up my comments and dashed to the men's room. It was a close call, but I made it. When I walked back into the chapel, the chaplain was saying "Amen"—but the crowd was cracking up. As I appeared, people started pointing at my microphone.

I was wearing a wireless mike, and it seems that I had left it on. The chaplain had been praying with my tinkling sounds in the background. Then the giggles had started. And just before he had pronounced the "Amen," I flushed. It was a very loud "Ka-Swoosh!" That had brought down the house. The congregation had a very good laugh at my expense.

DW was embarrassed driving around the track looking out his window and I was embarrassed having an audience while I was in the restroom, but both of those instances were harmless. It's quite another issue when we are embarrassed to come before God. When that happens, sin is involved.

Adam and Eve weren't embarrassed to be naked until they sinned. Their shame and awkwardness indicated a barrier that their sin had built between them and God. Their fig leaves were an outward sign that something had gone wrong.

We put barriers between us and God, our spouse, kids, friends and coworkers after we've wronged them. Then we hide rather than say "I'm sorry."

Have you put up barriers between people and you or God and you? Are you embarrassed being around them or embarrassed going to God in prayer? Do you need to say "I'm sorry" to anyone? How about God? Do you need to say "I'm sorry" to Him?

–GC

Forgiving Father, I want things to be right between us. Forgive me for my sins against You. Please show me the people I have wronged and give me the courage to ask forgiveness from them, too. Thank You.

TODAY'S READING: GENESIS 2:25–3:24; 1 JOHN 1:5-10;
PROVERBS 28:13; HOSEA 14:2

Along for the Ride

Understand, therefore, that the LORD your God is indeed God. He is the faithful God who keeps his covenant for a thousand generations and constantly loves those who love him and obey his commands.

DEUTERONOMY 7:9

One time a reporter asked Stevie, "Don't you get nervous when your husband is out there on the track going 200 miles an hour?" She replied, "No, not really, he's never gone *that* fast." Stevie had gotten used to the risk, but it was hard for her when we started. I'll let her tell what she went through.

I never felt like I really had a choice about what Darrell did. He was going to be a race-car driver. I thought I wanted to go along for the ride, but I remember our first Winston Cup race. I was scared.

I couldn't sleep the night before. I was tired and anxious. I said to the Lord, "If I'm going to do this for the rest of my married life, then I need You to help me respond on race day better than I am."

We needed someone to keep track of the laps and gas mileage, so I learned how and became part of the team. Keeping laps is a necessary job because you have to know when to bring the car in and how much gas you are going to need. The Lord gave me that job, and I was the only wife of a driver who did it.

I didn't wear a headset. There was too much rough talk on the headsets for my taste. So when the pit crew wanted to know something, someone would come and ask me, "How far can we go?" "How many laps have we gone?" "How many cautions have we had in this segment?" I kept track and answered questions for 25 years.

I always got nervous, but doing gas and laps helped me control the fear and focus on what Darrell was doing. Plus, I had the Christian singer Michael Card's CDs, so instead of listening to Darrell and the pit crew, I'd listen to Michael's music on my own headset. Michael Card became my friend.

Prayer, God and Michael have gotten me through some incredibly difficult days. My role on the race team is a testimony to the power of prayer, the faithfulness of God and the value of a friend.

–DW

The Old Testament recounts the story of a nameless poor single mom—a widow, actually—and her hungry son. There was a famine. She was almost ready to give up, but not quite. Single moms don't quit so easily.

The cupboards were bare. There was just enough flour and oil to make two small loaves of bread. She planned to prepare them and eat them with her son. After that, because there would be no more food, they would starve to death. This woman was rare. She loved Jehovah even though Queen Jezebel made it her business to kill God's prophets.[1]

Elijah came along. King James describes him, "He was an hairy man, and girt with a girdle of leather about his loins."[2] He sounds like a big hairy dude in a leather jock to me—and he was bald to boot. He had just spent the last six months hiding from Jezebel and being fed by ravens. That means he'd been living on road kill for half a year. He smelled like a backpacker. He said what God told him to say, but he sounded like a male chauvinist pig when he said it.

"Hey, woman, please get me a drink," he said to the nameless single mother. "And while you're at it, please bring me a piece of bread—from your hand."[3]

The scene was absurd. In the culture, she was second-class. She knew it and he knew it. Pharisees would later pray, "God, thank you that I am not a gentile, a dog, or a woman."[4] This was beyond abusive. However, the nameless single mother had been talking with God, and she had been listening.

After she told Elijah her story, he had the audacity to say, "Bake a loaf and give it to me. Then go make the second and split it with your son."[5]

Say what? Give you my starving son's food? No way! Her thoughts raced between the natural and the supernatural. This was a test. She made the right choice, preparing the bread for Elijah, who had also been listening to God. Afterward, the three of them ate for a long time.[6]

Like Stevie Waltrip, this remarkable woman learned about the power of prayer, the faithfulness of God and the value of a friend.

–*JC*

Tender shepherd, thank You for the gift of prayer and its power, thank You for Your faithfulness, thank You for friends and thank You for meeting my deepest needs. I'm so grateful. Amen.

TODAY'S READING: MATTHEW 6:33; PSALM 37:3-7; 1 THESSALONIANS 5:17; PHILIPPIANS 4:6-7; 1 KINGS 17:1-17

Over the Edge

*But to all who believed him and accepted him, he gave
the right to become children of God.*

JOHN 1:12

I was totally focused on racing. I did not want to get involved with anything that would take me away from being the best in my sport. Stevie had always supported me in my career. However, there came a day when she started hounding me to go to church. I resisted. I didn't want to be distracted.

We had a tough year in 1983. Stevie had her second miscarriage. I was involved in several serious wrecks, and I just missed winning the championship. God uses tough times to get our attention, and He got mine.

Having been raised in a Christian home, I assumed my soul was just fine. I had gone to Sunday School, said my prayers and always thought I was a good guy. I figured this was enough.

I don't remember who challenged me. Perhaps it was Max Helton, John "Bull" Bramlett (a former NFL linebacker-turned-preacher) or Dr. Cortez Cooper (my pastor)—or maybe it was all three of them. Over a period of time, these three guys got in my face: "Do you know where you're going to go when you die?" This was a wake-up call and a concept that brought me to Jesus, but there was another concept, too.

Most of the people I care about are deeply committed Christians. I started thinking, *If most of my friends and relatives are believers—if all of the people I love are believers—and are going to be in heaven and if I want to be with them again, then I had better make sure that I am going there, too.* This seemed like a pretty good reason to make a commitment.

I soon realized that being a church kid with Christian parents did not solve my problem, nor did being a good guy. In fact, while wanting to be with other Christians forever turned me in the right direction, it was actually not the ultimate answer either. It all came together for me one hot July night when I prayed a prayer with my pastor in a school that we were using for church. God pushed me over the edge.

–DW

Sooner or later we all reach the edge.

For the longest time I believed in evolution. It was all I had ever been taught. However, three observations changed my perception. The first was my discovery of the absence of transitional forms in the fossil records upon which the theory of evolution is hinged. Not only is the so-called missing link to man missing, it is also absent at all other supposed levels of lower life development. With this insight, I could only conclude that the origin of man couldn't have happened transitionally.

My second discovery was an understanding of the second law of thermodynamics. That law means that there are no perpetual motion machines. Everything winds down, not up. Smashed squirrels in the middle of the road never get better. They always become sail squirrels! (When flat and dried out you can take them by the tail and sail them like a Frisbee—I know, gross.) Meat spoils, fruit rots, and I'm getting old. Evolution has to move in violation of the second law of thermodynamics. That didn't make sense, and there is no proof that it has.

My third observation was based on mathematical odds. Mathematicians can establish probabilities from given variables. For example, the odds on the development of a polypeptide, which is a protein building block, is 6 times 10 to the 57th power, or 600 octodecillion, to 1. But a polypeptide is still miles away from a protein, let alone RNA or DNA.[1] Those odds are already ridiculous, but the probability of getting life into the proteins makes the whole concept impossible because it has to happen in the presence of protein-killing ultraviolet light. I concluded that none of this seemed remotely possible.

By contrast, when I found out the accuracy of the Bible and the fulfillment of the prophecies contained therein, I concluded it was not a book that happened by chance. Since God must be its author, and since its central theme is Jesus, receiving Christ was the next logical step. That's what pushed me over the edge. What pushed you over the edge? Do you know someone who needs a nudge?

–GC

*Creator God and author of saving grace, thank You for the ways
You've led me to Yourself, for showing Yourself to me and for tugging
on my heart. I'm so grateful. Amen.*

TODAY'S READING: JOHN 1:9-13; 3:31-36; COLOSSIANS 2:6-7

A Sure Thing

Jesus told him, "I am the way, the truth, and the life. No one can come to the Father except through me."

JOHN 14:6

If the map indicates that taking a particular road is the quickest way to get to the lake, that's the route I am taking. Some people suggest, "Why don't you go this way or that way?" and then proceed to tell me their secret short-cut or scenic route.

"No," I always say, "I don't have a lot of time, so the fastest way is the way I will go."

That is how I feel about heaven, too. I want to take the most direct path to get there. Why waste time looking at the clouds when I can be with Jesus? The Bible is like a map in that it shows us how to get there. It declares that there's only one way—and it is harder to get there than it is for a camel to go through the eye of a needle. I don't really need to analyze that and change it or fix it. I do not need to look for another way, because I have the map and I know the best route.

Jesus is the only way to get to heaven. I'm betting that's true. Even though it is tough, I am also betting that I will get there.

I look at it this way: If there's just a slight chance that Jesus is who He said He is, and if the Bible is His Word, what happens if we don't believe in Jesus when we die? The map shows that we will go to hell. Why would we take that chance? Why bet our souls on anyone other than Jesus?

Many people try to make getting to heaven more complicated than it really is. In racing we would take a procedure that was not broken, and then we would work on it until it was. A lot of people approach Jesus the same way. They work on their faith until it is broken. They try to figure out every-thing to the point of running in circles. It just makes more sense to go the simplest and most direct way. I bet the way to heaven is Jesus.

–DW

Place your bets," the table boss said as he gave the wheel a spin.

Four people pondered what to do. The first was a well-dressed, affluent, take-charge businessman. The second was a liberated New Age woman. The third was a religious man dressed in the tradition of his faith. And the fourth was an attractive woman dressed in a gown of humility and a scarf of repentance.

"You must place your bets," the table boss added with firmness. "Everybody has to wager."

The wealthy businessman wouldn't bet. The New Ager bet on reincarnation. The religious guy bet on any serious faith. And the last lady said, "I will bet on the Christ of the Bible. The Book has the least chance of being wrong."

The table boss said, "Ladies and gentlemen, as long as the wheel is spinning, you may change your minds. However, when it comes to a stop, all bets are final. Is that understood?"

All heads nodded, including the businessman's. He had come to the realization that not betting was, in fact, a bet.

All eyes riveted on the wheel. As it came to a stop, everyone knew the winners and losers.

It was then that the croupier reached under the table and opened the drawer. Smoke and sulfur belched upward, catching everyone off guard. Stench instantly filled the room. The table boss's gartered right arm flashed the hook in his hand across the table, catching three of the markers in its crook, and proceeded to rake them into the drawer. Three of the gamblers disappeared from the table. They had lost without realizing the foolishness of the terribly long odds they had chosen. The woman who bet on Jesus remained alone as the winner. At that moment she realized that she had not gambled at all. She had bet on a sure thing.

When the stakes are high, don't take needless risks. Never play a hunch. Never bet on what is popular or trendy. Play the odds.

Your soul is on the line. There is nothing more valuable than that. Since the Bible has stood the test of time, with Jesus as the central theme of the Bible, your best odds are with Christ. You can't beat a sure thing.

–*JC*

Forgiving Father, help me not to fall into the trap of tolerance.
I believe in free choice and in every person's right to believe whatever
he or she wants, but I don't have to believe everyone is right. You said there
is only one way. Thank You for the way to eternal life through
Jesus Christ, my Lord. I choose Him. Amen.

TODAY'S READING: JOHN 13:36–14:24; 1 JOHN 2:12; COLOSSIANS 2:13-14

Forever Changed

*Search me, O God, and know my heart; test me and know my
anxious thoughts. See if there is any offensive way in me,
and lead me in the way everlasting.*

PSALM 139:23-24, *NIV*

I was a church kid, but I didn't live that way. I gave Jesus lip service when I was 12, but nothing in me changed. I knew when I was doing something wrong, and I'd go and do it anyway. I lived that way for much of my adult years, too.

After Stevie put Jesus first in her life, she was on me about going to church. I raced on Sunday, and that was my excuse for not going. But I really did not want to face the music. Then a friend told us about a new church that held its meetings in a high school on Wednesday night—I lost my excuse. We went. Everything the pastor said seemed to be directed my way. God was getting my attention.

We were at church one July night in 1983. That season was not going well and my marriage was not going well. I was afraid for Stevie and me, and I was desperate enough to ask our pastor to pray for us.

Then I prayed. I asked the Lord to come into my life, come into my heart and get me out of the mess I was in. I told Him I was a sinner and asked Him to forgive me. He came to me that very night, and I got serious about my faith.

God didn't flip a switch; rather, my life slowly started to improve. There was no external change, but I was a different person. My attitude had changed. My outlook had changed. God had changed me, and my life truly took a huge 180-degree turn.

I think that night I was what we call born again, although my salvation may have happened when I was 12, and I had just been doing a good job at backsliding. No bells went off, no whistles sounded and I didn't win the prize behind door number two. There was no deal made between God and me, nor was it an if-you'll-do-this-I'll-do-that kind of thing. But I know that, at that moment, Jesus had become my Lord. From that day on, everything was different. I had been forever changed.

–DW

Unlike Darrell, I was not a church kid. My father was a bookie. He took bets on horse races and football games, and he ran the poker games in the back of a bar. My parents divorced when I was in the seventh grade, and my mom was a skid-row alcoholic.

My story is similar to Darrell's in that, when I was 14, I made a big decision. Here is what happened: I was hitchhiking. The man who picked me up asked me to go to church with him. I agreed and ended up going forward; I then prayed to receive Christ as my Savior. That day I also met the girl who would later become my wife, but not much else happened.

Years later, at 29, my marriage was in trouble. My wife and I had even discussed the possibility of divorce. We had started attending church again as a last-gasp attempt to save our marriage.

On our third Sunday at church, a man asked us to go to a conference for couples. I don't know what I thought the weekend would be like, but I never dreamed I'd end up spending most of it in church meetings.

The Saturday night speaker at the conference was Ken Poure. He talked about husband-and-wife stuff, like commitment, communication and biblical roles. He asked the men if we were dying for our wives as Christ had died for the Church.[1] When he finished, he said, "We're going to pray." Three people stood and prayed. Then my wife stood up. I could have killed her! I knew everyone would expect the ex-Laker (me) to pray next.

To my surprise, I stood. Convulsively crying, I prayed, "God, You made me; therefore, You must know what's best for me. I have proved that I don't. So I want to take my hands off my life and give control over to You. I don't know what that will mean, but I don't want to run it anymore. I don't want to say 'no' to You anymore. I know I will say it, but in my heart, I don't want to. If you can still use me, I'm yours."

God then healed my marriage and put me into Christian ministry. That was 33 years ago. Like DW, I had been forever changed.

–*GC*

Search me, O God, and know my heart; test me and know my anxious thoughts. See if there is any offensive way in me, and lead me in the way everlasting.[2]

TODAY'S READING: PSALM 139:23-24; EPHESIANS 2:1-9; TITUS 3:4-7; ROMANS 5:8; JOHN 1:12

Lost and Found

If our Message is obscure to anyone, it's not because we're holding back in any way. No, it's because these other people are looking or going the wrong way and refuse to give it serious attention.

2 CORINTHIANS 4:3, *THE MESSAGE*

After a race in Indianapolis, I needed to drive to the airport to catch a flight, so I loaded my family into the car and took off. The street that I normally took was closed. Since I did not know a detour, I started winding my way down streets in what I thought was the general direction of the airport. That was a bad decision. I got turned around and ended up on the wrong side of town.

When I realized my mistake, I turned around, but I refused to stop to ask for directions. Because the postrace traffic jammed the interstate, I took back roads. I got lost again. My kids, who were little at the time, were strapped into their car seats. We were all tired, and they began to scream. I was lost for two hours, but Stevie says it was four hours. I wouldn't stop for directions. I just couldn't.

On a different trip after another race, Stevie's dad, who was a big man, was stuffed in the backseat of my Camaro. I went the wrong way again. What was supposed to be a 30-minute trip turned into a nightmarish ordeal. Stevie's dad almost literally had smoke coming out his ears—he was so mad. I said, "Don't worry. I know I went the wrong way, but I know what I did wrong. We'll turn around and be there before you know it." It took us 45 minutes to get back to where we started, then a lot more time to get to where we were going.

It is odd how we do not want to ask for directions. Sometimes we know that we are lost; other times we do not even realize that we are on the wrong side of town. The same thing happens in marriages. Like any other couple, Stevie and I have our share of trouble. For the longest time I did not seek direction from God. I tried to get by on the back roads. God finally got my attention, but it took the possibility of losing my wife. Once He got into my head, I gave Him my heart. I had been lost, but then I was found.

—*DW*

Don Snow is an experienced outdoorsman. He often leads groups on hikes and overnight trips. I go backpacking with him when I can.

On one trip, Don and his group were cooking dinner when a family stumbled into their camp, shivering, thirsty and lost. Despite the obviousness of their plight, the dad flexed his machismo. The mom and the two teenaged boys were miserable and observably irritated. The happy family had climbed Mount Yale that day, but they had come down the wrong canyon and had been lost for more than five hours. They had not eaten since that morning and carried no water with them.

"Where's *a* trail?" asked Macho Dad, embarrassed.

Noticing the father had said "a trail," not "the trail," Don replied, "We'll have some food in about 10 minutes and a hot drink in about 5."

The woman and the boys nodded at the offer, but the dad would have nothing to do with it. "Just tell me where a trail is and how to get to Denny Creek trailhead," he scowled. The man was totally lost. Don had offered food and would have been willing to guide them down the canyon, but the father rejected the overtures. Why wouldn't he accept the help he and his family needed? Pride! He put himself, his wife and his children at risk because he was too proud.

It is one matter to get lost when driving a car. That only costs time. It is another matter when the entire family is off course, too. Consider a parent who is spiritually lost: Which way is he leading his wife and children? What about a single person or a teenager who has been going the wrong way but refuses to ask for directions? On what side of town will he or she end up? Have you been taking the side roads? Have you gone down the wrong canyon? Admit it. Confess it. Get some nourishment and the right directions. The Bible is a great road map.

–JC

Heavenly Father and trustworthy guide, help me in my stubbornness and pride. Forgive me for having gone my own way. I want to turn to You for direction in this life, and I want to enjoy being with You forever. May everything that I do bring You glory. Thank You.

TODAY'S READING: LUKE 15:3-10; PSALM 51:10-13; 2 CORINTHIANS 3:12—4:7

 Tuning In

And do not bring sorrow to God's Holy Spirit by the way you live. Remember, he is the one who has identified you as his own, guaranteeing that you will be saved on the day of redemption.

EPHESIANS 4:30

In racing, instincts are just about everything. As drivers, we need all of our senses working. We need sight, touch, smell and sound. When we're driving the car and something's happening to it, we can smell it. We can hear it in the changing tone of the engine.

I almost always knew when my car was going to blow up because I could feel it. If my car was starting to go, all of my senses would come alive.

Many times when I went into the pits, the crew chief would ask, "What's wrong?"

I would say, "It's gettin' ready to blow up."

"What?" He would say, not believing me. "Are you sure?"

I would say it again: "It's gettin' ready to blow up."

"How do you know?" he would repeat, still not believing.

I have driven for a lot of people who wouldn't believe me. I would have to let the car blow up before they would see. But it costs a lot of money to let a car blow up because we usually wreck when we do that and we can get hurt.

Many times I've had the crew pull an engine out of a car when it was running fine. I would say, "I don't know what's wrong, 'cuz I'm not down in there with it, but I know somethin' is wrong." They would pull the engine, take it home, and later say, "Well, you were right. We were scuffing a piston," or "The thing is losing a lobe on a camshaft" or "The rod bearings were just getting ready to fly out of the thing."

When we are in tune with the car, it speaks to us with a small voice. I always knew when something wasn't right. On the track, I always had to use all of my senses. I even needed the sense of taste—we have to taste victory if we are ever going to win.

—*DW*

The Old Testament recounts story after story that reveal how God spoke to people. Sometimes He talked loudly and was accompanied by lightning and thunder, or with emphasis like creating a crevasse for Korah and his bunch.[1] But He sometimes talked to people directly. With Moses, it was face-to-face, but He also had conversations with Aaron, Miriam, Noah, Abraham and all the prophets. Sometimes He used words, but most of the time he communicated through visions and dreams.

In the New Testament, it is recorded that God spoke to Elizabeth, Zacharias, Mary and Joseph. He talked to the people gathered at Jesus' baptism and to Paul on the Damascus Road. God spoke the book of Revelation to John. And yes, since Jesus was both God and man, when He talked, it was God talking. However, after the Holy Bible was assembled, it seems that God chose to amend the way He would communicate.

These days He certainly can speak in many ways, but it seems to me that He most often speaks through His Word and in a small voice—even a whisper—and He uses the Third Person of the Trinity to do it. That's right, the Holy Spirit. Because of His physical body and its restrictions, Jesus was limited as to how many people He could address or touch. But the Holy Spirit is not limited.

Whereas in the Old Testament the Holy Spirit spoke to a few people and enabled them in special ways, in the New Testament, after Pentecost, the Spirit became available to everyone. From that point on, if a person knew Jesus Christ as Savior and Lord, the Holy Spirit dwelled in him or her. Sin grieves and quenches His voice, but obedience turns up the volume—or at least enables us to hear the small voice.

To hear the Holy Spirit, we have to get in tune with Jesus. And the better we know Christ and live like Him, the clearer the voice of the Spirit becomes. It's a lot like DW's driving a race car. When he knows his car, what it tells him can keep him from wrecking. This is an illustration of what happens when we get to know Jesus. When we listen intently to the Holy Spirit, we won't wreck as much.

–*JC*

Holy God in heaven, I want to be so in tune with Your Holy Spirit that I do not miss a sound. Incline my ear to listen closely. May how I live my life turn up the volume and not grieve or quench Your power. Amen.

TODAY'S READING: NUMBERS 12:1-9; 16:1-35; MATTHEW 3:13-17; 1 THESSALONIANS 5:12-22; EPHESIANS 4:25—5:2

Staying out of Trouble

Be not far from me, for trouble is near; for there is none to help.

PSALM 22:11, *NASB*

I can be an inch away from the car in front of me and not even be looking at it. In a race, we set a pace; then we run in traffic following that pace. We don't have to look over the end of our own hood to see the car in front of us; rather, we look through the windows of that car to see what is going on in front of it. We always look as far ahead as we possibly can. We look for trouble. If we are coming down the back straightaway of the racetrack and we see smoke in the corner ahead, we know there is a problem. When this happens, we raise a hand to alert the drivers around us so that they know that we are slowing down. We always have to remember that the driver behind us isn't watching us; he's looking past us. If we slow down when he doesn't expect it, he's going to bump us.

We don't have brake lights, so we must use hand signals. There are signals for slowing down, really slowing down, let's go, hold and let's work together. We try to cue each other, especially when there is trouble ahead. Ninety-five percent of the time drivers will hold with each other, but every now and then some driver will decide, *Hey, you're gonna' hold, I'm gonna' go.* If there is trouble, it's better to let him go but hold back yourself—always play it safe.

We are constantly working with the other drivers around us, particularly at the bigger racetracks where we draft. We will be thinking, *Come on, buddy, let's stick together. If we work together, we can catch that guy up there.* On a track such as Daytona or Talladega, two or three cars drafting together can go a second per lap faster than the driver running by himself out in front. If the second- and third-place drivers work together, they can catch up with the leader.

–DW

Darrell's hand signals are one way to communicate volumes without saying a word. Concepts or metaphors are ways to communicate a whole body of information with a few well-chosen words.

I used the conceptual approach in my book *Counterattack: Taking Back Ground Lost to Sin*. Here are some examples: A "polar-bear alert" helps us take our thoughts captive. "Keep the penny under the wheel" helps us overcome sexual temptation. "Keeping the éclairs out of your refrigerator" prevents us from living against our prayers. It's a wonderful way to teach.

When my wife, Mary, and I go to Maui to visit our son, we attend Kumulani Chapel. The pastor is a wonderful, intense young man named Scott Craig. He got my interest right away because he too uses figurative language to communicate concepts. He will say things such as "Burn your ships," "Check your guns at the door" and "Keep your antennae up."

I like "burn your ships" a lot. It can be applied to many aspects of faith. When the explorer Hernan Cortes landed in Mexico, he burned his ships. His men could not retreat. They had no choice but to go forward.

"Check your guns at the door" can mean that when we walk into a gathering, we must check our ego at the door and enter in humility, with the attitude of a servant, and regard others as more important.

"Keep your antennae up" refers to staying alert for God's leading in any given situation.

Mary and I have been having fun with these sayings. When one of us starts to get in a funk, the other will say, "Burn the ships." We're tired of doing things the old way. If someone cuts us off on the freeway one of us will say, "Check your guns at the door." The entire concept of anger management is embraced in that single metaphor. When leaving the house to meet with friends, we'll remind each other to raise our spiritual antennae. We never know when God might want to do something.

–GC

Almighty God and heavenly Father, direct my vision forward. Keep me out of trouble. Don't allow me to wander to the right or the left. As a new creation in Christ, don't let me go back to my old ways. Help me to value others more than I currently do. And Lord, I want to be sensitive to Your leading. Thank You.

TODAY'S READING: 2 CORINTHIANS 5:11-19; GALATIANS 6:11-16;
COLOSSIANS 3:12-17; PSALM 22:11

A Miracle

In the name of Jesus Christ of Nazareth, get up and walk!

ACTS 3:6

When I got T-boned at Daytona in 1990, I had a concussion and the entire left side of my body was broken: all of my ribs, my thigh and my arm at the elbow. The X rays were convincing. Doctors wrapped my ribs, put a titanium plate with screws in my leg and placed my arm in a cast. I was a mess.

All I could think about was getting out of the hospital so that I could run a lap at Pocono. I needed to run the lap so that I could stay in the running for points. When the doctor came into my hospital room, I reached up and with both hands I grabbed the bar above my bed. I tried to raise myself up a bit and push myself back so that I could sit up. The doctor had a fit. He hollered, "Don't do that to your arm! You can't—you shouldn't even be able to do that. How did you do that?"

I smiled and said, "Well, I'm telling you, there's nothing wrong with my arm. If you take this cast off, I'll show you. I swear there's nothing wrong. My arm is fine. It doesn't hurt a bit."

He had the nurses take off the cast and take me down get it X-rayed. The break wasn't there. The arm was fine. Between Friday, when I went in the hospital and had the first X rays taken, and Monday, it had been healed. That was a miracle. Stevie was convinced that God had answered prayer. Because the arm was fine, I was able to use crutches to start rehab. Otherwise, I would have been in a wheelchair.

The doctor had a difficult time believing God had healed me. He was overwhelmed. "Well, occasionally this happens," he said. Then he tried to rationalize it away: "The arm must have been turned wrong or something and it just appeared to be broken. It had to have been a mistake. Maybe there was a hair on the machine or something."

The doctor did not know what had happened, but I did. My arm had been healed. I couldn't use it on Friday, but I could lift my weight with it on Monday. In my book, that's a miracle.

–DW

When I think of the 1,500 or so years of Old Testament history, I'm amazed at how few specific miracles are actually recorded. The working power of the hand of God is everywhere, but there aren't all that many accounts of miracles. I have counted 67. Of those, Moses and Aaron were involved in 21. Elijah was there for seven. Elisha witnessed 27, and four others saw the remainder. That is only eight key people for all of the Old Testament miracles.

Jesus did at least 37 miracles in three years all by Himself—that is all that are recorded. Of the others that are mentioned, Peter saw 5. Paul witnessed 20. Philip, Stephen and the 70 returning disciples were involved with some. The 30-year period covered by Acts is filled with miraculous signs and wonders, but most of them are at the beginning of the book. There aren't very many at the end. Paul can't even fix his eye problem and Timothy can't fix his stomach ulcers. The way I see it, miracles declined, but I don't think they ever ceased.

In the New Testament, God used miracles to demonstrate His power.[1] Paul loved to show up in a new town and find a crippled man everyone knew.[2] Paul would pray and God would heal him. Then the guy would run all over town and draw a big crowd. Paul would preach and people, having seen the miracle, would hear the Word and believe.

Some theologians conclude that when the final books of the Bible came together, God stopped doing miracles because He could now speak to people through His Holy Word.[3] There are others who believe it is a miracle when they get the last parking space in a busy shopping mall. I don't know about the miracle of the parking space, but there is no question in my mind that God continues to heal. It's happening in the inner cities, in third-world countries and in hospitals like the one DW was in.

On Friday, DW couldn't use his arm because it was broken. On Monday he lifted his body weight with the same arm. Call it what you will, but God made that possible. DW and I call it a miracle.

—GC

Dear God of signs and wonders, help me with my unbelief and strengthen my faith. Do what it takes to draw me near to You. I want to walk with You, talk with You and experience all I can of You all the days of my life. Thank You.

TODAY'S READING: ACTS 3:1-26 (THE CHURCH'S FIRST MIRACLE); 14:8-17; DEUTERONOMY 4:2; PROVERBS 30:6; REVELATION 22:18-19

The End of Myself

Though he slay me, yet will I hope in him.

JOB 13:15, *NIV*

My worst road trip was in 1990 at Pocono. It was two weeks after I had been T-boned in Daytona. My arm was healed but I still had broken ribs and a titanium plate holding my shattered thigh together. I was in more pain than just a little bit. Since I was in the top 10 in points for the championship, there was no way anyone could keep me from going to Pocono to start that race. My plan was to drive one lap and then change drivers. Under NASCAR rules I would still get the points.

I had a special brace made for my leg. I was on crutches. I was swollen and in no condition to be doing any driving, even though I convinced my doctor I could. I dropped from 195 pounds to 170 pounds. The leg could bend enough to work a real soft, short-throw clutch in the car. I figured that I could move my arm enough to work the gears to make one lap. If I could get a lift through the window and get in the seat, I thought it might work.

Just before the trip to Pocono, Stevie had hurt her neck and the doctor had given her something for it. She has allergies, but he assured her that the medication would not cause a reaction.

The race wasn't until Sunday, but I had to do a lap on Saturday to prove I could drive. We got in the airplane Friday afternoon to get there a day early. The weather was bad—thunderstorms were everywhere. It was bumpy, it was thunderin' and lightnin' and we were bouncing around. I was in pain and I could not stand the bouncing. We finally got to Pennsylvania, but it was 11 P.M. before we got to bed.

An hour later Stevie poked me and said, "I don't feel right." I thought, *You don't feel right? You ought to be over here where I am*. But I bit my tongue and said, "Well, what's wrong, Honey?" She answered, "There's somethin' wrong with me."

Stevie turned on the light and I about jumped out of bed. Her lips were turned inside out. Her eyes were swollen shut. Her face was big and puffy. She had broken out in hives. I didn't even recognize her. She'd had a reaction to the medicine. I called for help because I couldn't move, and we went to the hospital emergency room.

The next day, I was told by NASCAR to start at the rear, and I wasn't supposed to pass anyone. But on Sunday, some guys were lagging and I passed them. I got penalized a lap. I yelled and screamed, standing there on my crutches, and it was a mess. Our team had already been struggling. We'd been blaming each other.

Weeks earlier I had said, "It can't get any worse." Then I got T-boned, and I woke up in the hospital and it got worse. Again I said, "It can't get any worse." Then we went to Pocono and it got worse. After that I said, "I'm never gonna say 'It can't get any worse again' 'cuz it can always get worse."

That was the trip from hell. On the way home, I looked at Stevie and she was still puffed up. I was all broken up and beat up. I felt a little bit like Job must have felt, and I cried.

God was pulling the props out from under me so that I would turn to Him for support. But I was stubborn, as it took a few more years for me to get to the end of myself.

—DW

———————

Darrell had it good compared to what Job went through. It started when a hired hand told him some bad guys had stolen the donkeys and killed the workers. *That's bad*, he thought. *Things can't get any worse than this.* Another arrived to say that lightning had killed all the sheep and the herdsmen who had been attending them. *That's real bad*, he thought. *Things can't get any worse than this.* Still another messenger said that renegades had stolen the camels and killed the herdsmen. *That's terrible*, he thought. *Things can't get any worse than this.* But the next guy said a tornado had killed Job's children. And things had gotten worse. I think he cried.

God restored Job and he restored Darrell, but not until they got to the end of themselves. When we're whining, we're not at the end. When we're at the end, we cry.

—GC

I came naked from my mother's womb, and I will be stripped of everything when I die. The Lord has given me everything that I have, and the Lord may take it away. Praise the name of the Lord! For whatever happens in my life, I will not sin by blaming God. Amen.[1]

TODAY'S READING: JOB 1:1-22; 13:15; MATTHEW 6:10; 26:39

Staying in the Garden

O my son, give me your heart. May your eyes
delight in my ways of wisdom.

PROVERBS 23:26

We are all so vulnerable. Something or someone tempts each one of us every day, and it's hard to keep our guard up all the time. Sometimes it is like being in a candy store, or maybe it is more like being in the Garden of Eden with the serpent pointing toward the forbidden fruit. It is particularly tough when you are a popular sports figure. I have to admit, I've got a really neat deal goin' here. And sometimes that fruit looks very tempting.

As enticing as the temptations may be, I made up my mind some time ago that I am no longer going to sow wild oats. I challenged myself to ask myself *Are you so weak that you don't have enough—as my mom would say—gumption about you that you can't honor a commitment?*

I made a commitment to quit drinking. Now every time I sit down, if somebody's having a glass of wine, I have to tell myself, *No, I'm not going to do that.* I know that it's just a glass of wine, but I also know how I am. Before I stopped drinking beer and wine, I never could drink just one. I had to have five or six. I never was an alcoholic and I never was a drunk, but I had the genes. Drinking runs in my family.

If I'm offered a great glass of Merlot, I can't help but start to rationalize *It would smell good, taste good and it's good for my heart.* I'll get almost there and then my faithful Father will remind me, and I'll think, *No, no, no! I don't want to get kicked out of the Garden.* I'd rather keep my commitment.

In my sport, Winston sponsored NASCAR, and Budweiser sponsored my car, so I used to say, "Smokin' and drinkin' got us where we are today." But we also know smoking and drinking can get us where we don't want to be. If we have a weakness for something and know it, we'd be better off to leave it alone.

I'm real close to God now, and I wouldn't trade this relationship for anything. With His help, I won't taste the candy in the candy store and I'll stay in the Garden.

–DW

Impulsively we walk or mouse-click our way into a candy store and start to reach for the forbidden fruit. My downfall is a Dairy Queen Snickers Blizzard with a double scoop of Snickers. It tastes good, but can I always trust my senses?

Consider this: Pilots face a dilemma when flying through a bank of clouds or thick fog. I'd heard that a plane could be in a shallow dive and the pilot wouldn't know it, so I asked a pilot about flying in such conditions. He told me that dominant, decisive people have the most difficult time in the cockpit. Their instincts tell them one thing and the instruments tell them another. Despite the readings on the gauges, they insist that they are flying straight and level because they're used to trusting their own instincts. How do the other pilots handle such people? "We don't worry about it much," he told me. "They tend to weed themselves out very quickly." It seems that pilots who survive are the ones who trust the gauges.

God gave us the gauges. In the Bible, He makes it clear that if there is a conflict between what we think is right and what the Bible says is right, the choice that's right isn't usually the Bible—it's always the Bible!

When I was 29, I made a decision that saved my marriage and probably saved my life. I decided that if God would show me what He wanted, I would do my best to do it. I understood that I might mess up with spontaneous behavior, but I vowed that given time to decide, I would do my best to do what Jesus would do.

I drove a nail that day upon which I would hang the rest of my life decisions. That nail has kept me from my own foolishness and has kept me from following my own instincts. Do you need to make a decision to drive a nail upon which you will hang the rest of your life decisions? Choose this day what you will do when you find yourself in a candy store.[1] Decide this day if you want to follow your instincts or stay in the Garden.

–GC

Oh, Lord, I choose this day to make the rest of my life decisions on the basis of the truth of Your Holy Word, the Bible. Help me to learn Your Word and be consistent in my decisionmaking. May You receive the glory. Amen.

TODAY'S READING: MATTHEW 8:18-22; ROMANS 12:1; PROVERBS 23:26; 22:17-18; 23:12

Sympathy Pains

Bear one another's burdens, and thereby fulfill the law of Christ.

GALATIANS 6:2, NASB

When Stevie was pregnant with our first child, I got morning sickness, too. I even threw up with her. My body wanted to help bear her burden, I guess. That's pretty weird, isn't it?

But the wives of race-car drivers are weird, too. They have to be to be married to us. There was a time when Stevie got sympathy pains for me, too. Her anguish was real. She knew she wasn't hurt, and that what she felt wasn't from anything that had happened to her, but it was genuine pain and it wouldn't go away. She couldn't even take a deep breath.

It happened in 1995. I was racing really well, until I got hurt. I broke all the ribs under my right shoulder blade in the back. Nonetheless, I insisted upon racing the next time out because I wanted to maintain my place in the point standings or move up.

I did not realize how much my body hurt until I got buckled into my car seat for the qualifying run. I couldn't shift. I had to reach across with my other hand to get the car in gear. As I came off turn four, I almost wrecked. I could barely control the vehicle and I had to come in. I couldn't drive that day. Stevie, though not hurt, was feeling the pain, too.

Doc Brewer was at the track and came to see me. He had tobacco juice running out of the corner of his mouth. After checking me over he said, "If you're gonna qualify tonight, you're gonna have to numb those ribs. You want me to do it?" I did, so he gave me two shots. I qualified ninth but didn't think that I could race the next day. I thought I would go one lap, and then let a relief driver take over. Stevie was still hurting.

On race day, I surprised everyone and went 80 laps. Stevie later told me, "When you got out of the car, my pain went away. That's pretty weird, isn't it? You got morning sickness when I was pregnant, and I got sympathy pains when you drove hurt. I guess we are really into bearing each other's burdens."

–DW

I did not have morning sickness when my wife was pregnant, but right now I'm having sympathy pains of another kind. I'm hurting for the American troops in the Middle East and for the families of those who have loved ones in harm's way. The hurt hit home when I was in Colorado Springs to speak to the United States Air Force cadets.

In Colorado Springs, I watched four squadrons of men and women in full dress for Friday-night lowering of the flag. It's called retreat. The Drum and Bugle Corps played the national anthem while the flag was lowered. I stood a little taller, my chest was out a little further, and there was a lump in my throat. With the playing of taps came tears, unchecked and without shame.

The fiancée of a future pilot stood in front of me. She understood the somber mood as we honored flag and country. The cadet to my right understood, too. A dad and two kids who didn't understand played and talked off to my left.

The flag was folded, and the squadrons marched off to the playing of "God Bless America." I watched it all—until each squadron had broken ranks at their respective dorms. I'll never forget that moment. I wiped my face and then spent four days talking to 80 cadets who loved Jesus.

These men and women were preparing to bear the burdens that come with preserving freedom. As I write, men and women are giving their lives for that cause in the Middle East.

A Native American concept of what the English word "friend" means is better defined as "one who carries my sorrows on his back."[1] In Galatians, the apostle Paul instructed us to bear one another's burdens. That doesn't mean to carry the whole load but, rather, to help carry the load if it is becoming too much. He was not only talking about helping each other, but he was also talking about having sympathy pains.

Our military is bearing the primary burden of preserving freedom, and I'm having sympathy pains for them. I can't physically help bear their burdens, but I can pray more. May God bless the troops and may God bless America.

–GC

Almighty God, please put Your hand of blessing on our troops and on our leaders. Give them courage, wisdom and strength as they carry the burden of the preservation of peace. Father God, would You bless our country and keep us in the palm of Your mighty hand while You bring peace in the Middle East. Thank You.

TODAY'S READING: GALATIANS 6:1-5; ROMANS 12:9-21; 15:1-6

For the Children

And further, you will submit to one another out of reverence for Christ.

EPHESIANS 5:21

I don't know how a 60-year-old or 70-year-old man can leave his wife, especially for a younger woman. I have known men who have done it. She's 30-something; He's 70-something. He is going to get sick or die pretty soon. What's he going to do when he can't take care of himself? Is that younger woman going to take care of him like his wife of 40 or 50 years would have? I don't think so. I haven't walked in those shoes—and no one can know until he does walk in another man's shoes—but I still don't get it.

To say that I've never thought about leaving my wife isn't true. I've thought about divorce many times. Once, when we didn't have anything keeping us together except a house and a car, I thought, *You can have those. I'm out of here.* We were pretty close to splitting around the time I prayed to make Christ first in my life. That prayer probably saved our marriage.

Life changed once our daughters came along. Suddenly it was not just two of us, but there were three and then four of us. We have seen my sister get divorced a couple of times. Stevie's sister has divorced. All of the kids are scarred by it. Divorce tears up kids. They never understand. They don't get it. And they always take some responsibility they shouldn't. Kids always assume the blame. They don't get over it.

I think when a person makes a commitment he or she has got to do everything in his or her power to stick to it. It's the same way on the race-track. Indecisiveness gets people hurt. When a driver makes an unexpected move, it might not mess him up, but it messes somebody else up. It can wreck the driver behind him and leave a mess in the wake. That is how it is in marriage. A person has made a commitment to his or her spouse and kids. All of a sudden, that person makes an unexpected move and wants out. The spouse who leaves may be able to go on his or her merry way, but look at what breaking the commitment does to the people around him or her.

–DW

I was talking to a 95-year-old man. He was getting a divorce. I asked him, "Why would you throw away 75 years of marriage?"

He replied, "Well, it hasn't been good for a long time but we wanted to wait until the kids died."

That's a joke, but God bless them for staying together for the sake of the kids. Children are a great reason to keep a commitment.

I come from a broken home. My folks drank a lot and then fought a lot. They both slept around too. I came to fear parties, because there would always be a fight after everyone went home. I was even awakened once to find my dad beating up my mom's lover in the middle of the living room floor. Imagine a fifth grader jumping into the fray trying to help. My parents finally divorced when I was in the seventh grade. I still feel the pain of my childhood, but nothing hurt more than them finally flicking it in. As bad as it was when they were together, there is no question in my mind that I would have done better if they had stayed together. The divorce sent me into a major tailspin. I vowed that I would never do that to my kids.

By the early 1970s, I had married my high school sweetheart and had two kids. I didn't care much about God at that time in my life, and my marriage was going badly. We both had used the d word with each other—we had both talked about getting a divorce. There is only one reason that we stayed together long enough to let the Lord get a hold of us. I had made a vow to make sure my kids never went through what I had gone through, and Mary and I both wanted to keep our commitment to each other, even though we didn't like each other very much at the time. We agreed that we ought to do what is best for the children.

What's best for the children? Asking the question resolves the problem of easy divorce. Many studies show that, unless there is a dangerous situation, children from divorced homes don't do as well in all areas of life as those from whole homes. If you are married, stay together. Kids shouldn't be left wrecked in anyone's rearview mirror.

–JC

Heavenly counselor, protector and Father, help me to protect the children in our world. Show me how to make them more important than my own well-being. And dear Lord, protect the institution of marriage, both for Your sake and for the sake of our nation. Thank You.

TODAY'S READING: PSALMS 127:3-5; 144:12;
LUKE 9:46-48; 18:15-17; EPHESIANS 6:4

It's About Time

Make the most of every opportunity for doing good.

EPHESIANS 5:16

In my sport, time is everything. Whoever covers the distance in the shortest amount of time will be first across the finish line. Some would think that being fast is the key, and that's important, but speed on the track isn't the only thing. You can have the fastest car and not win the race. Races are often won and lost in the pits.

Choreography, specialization and technology have improved pit-stop times considerably. When I was racing in the 1980s, it took 22 seconds to change four tires and take on 22 gallons of gas. Now it can be done in 14 seconds. Time is everything.

Well-known people have a big problem with time: There is so little of it. People are always making demands on us. Now that I am in the broadcast booth, I am better known than when I was racing. Our sport is much more popular today than it used to be. More than 17 million homes listen to what I have to say on race day.[1] All that exposure increases the demands on my time. There are unending requests to speak and to take part in events that are mostly all worthwhile. How to sort out good, bad, better and best, and do what's right, and still have a family life are very difficult. I got a better grip on solving the problem with the help of a coach.

Joe Gibbs is the coach of the Washington Redskins and owner of the Joe Gibbs Racing Team. He says, "Everyone needs a coach." Coach Gibbs is my time-management coach. I was having trouble with all the demands on me. I asked him how he handles his situation. He said, "I'd rather talk to five unsaved people than five hundred who already know the Lord."

Coach Gibbs's approach helped me utilize my time better. There is only so much of it, so I want it to count. I don't preach to the choir anymore. We've been commissioned to spread the gospel, so I concentrate on lost souls.

–DW

Nehemiah was well known in his day and certainly had great demands on his time. If he had been an athlete, he might have gotten a Nike contract. When it came to time management, he certainly lived by the maxim Just do it.

It took Nehemiah and his crew just 52 days to rebuild the walls and make and hang new gates in Jerusalem.[2] It was a world record! Nehemiah proved that it is possible to do great things with God when we stay focused— one of the most important aspects of using our time wisely.

Nehemiah had enemies who wanted to keep the Jewish people underfoot. To assure that his crew could work unimpeded, he armed the workers and positioned watchmen. He was determined not to allow for any distractions and once quipped, "I am doing a great work! I cannot stop to come and meet with you."[3] When his enemies spread lies about his character, he still kept his focus and pressed on. The work was more important than his reputation, and God's perception of him meant more than that of men and women. Nehemiah stayed focused and made the most of his time.

People who excel in business know how important focus is to success. Former Chrysler chairman Lee Iacocca once said, "If you want to make good use of your time, you've got to know what's most important and then give it all you've got."[4] That is another way of saying "Just do it."

I can tell what's important to people by how they spend their time. How much time do you spend in front of the television? How much time online? How much time is spent on your hobby? We all have 24 hours with which to glorify our Lord. How are you using your time? Are you rescuing it from waste?

Rebuilding Jerusalem was important to Nehemiah, so that is how he used his time. Telling people about Jesus is important to Darrell, and that is how he uses his time. How do you use yours?

–*JC*

Great creator of time and space, help me to be a better manager of the 24 hours allotted to me each day and help me to focus on the things to which You have called me. May You be glorified with my time, and may my time be Yours. Thank You.

TODAY'S READING: EPHESIANS 5:15-17; GALATIANS 3:13; MATTHEW 6:19-21; NEHEMIAH 1—6:15 (FOR THE WHOLE STORY)

Bologna Sandwiches

We may throw the dice, but the LORD determines how they fall.

PROVERBS 16:33

Some athletes will not compete unless they are wearing their lucky socks. I don't like to use the word "lucky." That's superstition. But when I was racing, I did have favorites. I had a favorite uniform, favorite shoes, favorite helmet and favorite car. The pieces of duct tape with Scripture written on them that Stevie put in the car at the beginning of each race meant a lot to me, too.

I ate a bologna sandwich before each race, while everybody else was eating steak and chicken. I had many routines, but I didn't see them as superstitious rituals. Routines helped prepare me to race, but I don't believe we can mystically manipulate variables. Attempting to do that crosses the line into magic.

No one can predict what is going to happen in a race. We can look at the results of the last race or of similar races over the last 10 years. Such a review helps us know what to expect. But we have no way of knowing what is actually going to happen. Think about all of the variables: the engine running at maximum power, the tires, the suspension, all the parts on the car, driving the car on the edge, the pits, and changing conditions and temperatures. These are just the variables for one driver. To get the full picture multiply it all by 43.

A race usually lasts four hours—a lot of time for something to go wrong. Rather than good or bad luck, so much of what happens is just the breaks. Sometimes we get them and sometimes we don't, but there is nothing we can do to make them go our way, except to be as prepared as we can possibly be. I knew I was having a good day when I was on the backstretch and everything bad was happening on the front stretch, or when I needed to make a pit stop and the caution flag came out, allowing me to stop without losing any time. I would always be amazed when I would finish 500 miles and nothing bad had happened.

Life can be compared to racing. There are so many variables. We can plan, but we never know what's going to happen.

–DW

Most athletes are into routines. Some have rituals. Most would call these terms synonyms, but they are not. One has God's approval and one does not.

If athletes have played well in the previous game, they will try to do everything prior to the next contest the same way they did it before the last one. As gross as it sounds, some guys never wash their lucky whatever. Others have to have their floppy socks. Coaches wear their "winning" coats, or charms, or carry their good-luck somethings. Attempts to influence luck are rituals and are based on superstition.

Some athletes don't want anyone to talk to them during their pregame preparation. They are focusing. Some won't stop talking. They are focusing, too. The legendary basketball coach John Wooden always rolled up his program and turned to wave at his wife just before tip-off. Always! It was his way of focusing. Those are routines.

Shooting free throws requires preparation and focus. Have you ever noticed some of the outlandish sequences some players go through? How about five bounces, a wrap around the waist, spin the ball on the palm, take a deep breath and fire? Karl Malone always talks to himself before he shoots his freebies. Jason Kidd blows a kiss to his family. Some of that is routine, but most is just for show.

An athlete may say "I had a bad game," but many don't really believe it was their fault. Some external circumstance must be to blame: "Mom washed my jock." "The equipment manager forgot my socks." "I put my jersey on before I put on my shorts." I know it sounds strange, but many athletes think that way. That's either superstition or immaturity or both.

Let's clear the air on this one. Routines and rituals may make a player more consistent in his or her performance, but neither influences external variables. Routines may calm, focus and help performance, but rituals assume a spiritual outcome, and that's the difference between the two concepts.

Routines are meant to help a person's performance. Rituals are meant to influence external circumstances. Routines become rituals when we hope they will change our luck by altering situations beyond our control. Rituals are just another way of praying to false gods—and we know what God thinks about that.

–*JC*

Heavenly Father, I don't want to worship false idols or spirits. I don't want to try to influence factors in life over which I have no control. May all my prayers be directed to You. Amen.

TODAY'S READING: PROVERBS 16:33; 18:18; ACTS 1:15-26; 19:13-20;
ROMANS 8:28; REVELATION 21:5-8

A fan favorite. On his way to three Driver of the Year awards and the Driver of the Decade honor (in the 1980s), Darrell often drove car number 17 (below) and built up a huge following. He even joked with the media (left) after winning the pole position of a race.

On the right track. In his later years of racing, DW and Stevie would always pray before the engines started (above, top). Pastor Cortez Cooper has been a mentor and friend to Darrell and Stevie (above, center). DW hosts a weekly men's Bible study at his house in Tennessee (right).

The Focus Factor

*"Get out of here, Satan," Jesus told him. "For the Scriptures say,
'You must worship the Lord your God; serve only him.'"*

MATTHEW 4:10

To be good, race-car drivers must be focused. Everything happens fast at over 180 miles an hour. If we look over at the guy in the next car for an instant, we will drift sideway several feet. If the car is too loose, the rear end will start to come around and the car will start to spin. If it is too tight, the front wheels lose their bite and the car might go up and into the wall. If we do not pay attention, we will never make the necessary corrections to counter whatever is going on. If we lose our focus, we lose control and may wreck.

Carbon monoxide is a big problem at some tracks. Our cool box helps filter it out, but by the end of a race it is not unusual to have a splitting headache. Drivers are in the car three and a half hours and have no opportunity to visit the boys' room. We have to be careful that we do not become dehydrated from the intense heat in the car. We can't drink enough to stay hydrated. These are all major distractions, and distractions can cause us to lose focus.

I've had a lot of broken bones over the years. I've smashed my shoulders, ribs, collarbones, legs and arms. Pick a body part and I have probably shattered it. One time after I got an MRI, the doctor said, "In addition to the leg and the arm, you have seven broken ribs. And did you know that you've broken all your ribs over the course of the years?"

I answered, "Thank God I didn't do them all at once."

My mom taught me to be tough, though. As kids, when we got hurt she'd say, "Dry it up. You'll live!" That helped me when I got older, because I could still drive when I was dinged up. I could keep my focus even when I was driving with broken bones.

Race-car drivers who can't stay focused for the entire race usually don't finish, and even when they do, they never finish well. On the track, it is vital that we keep our focus on the big picture, no matter what is going on around us.

—DW

It is important to keep our focus in life, too.

A four-year-old got the point, but her dad missed it. The little girl was learning to look both ways before going out into the street. One day there was a freshly hit, dead squirrel, with its guts spread out where the little girl was about to step off the curb. Her dad said, "Oh, that's too bad. I'll bet a car was going too fast."

"Maybe," said the child, "but the squirrel didn't look both ways."

She got it! Dad didn't.

An alcoholic was sitting at a bar trying to figure out where he would get his next drink. A do-gooder came by, jabbered about the evils of hard liquor and then put two glasses in front of the drunk. The reformer proceeded to pour three inches of bourbon into one of the glasses and three inches of water into the other. Then he pulled out a little tin, opened it and pulled out two worms. As he stared into the glassy eyes of the intoxicated man, the crusader dropped a worm in each glass. The old drunk watched the worm in the glass of alcohol shrivel up and die, while the other seemed to flourish and frolic in the water. "What does that tell you?" asked the man, hoping to preach the benefits of sobriety.

"If you have worms, you better drink a lot," was the drunk's reply.

He didn't get it! The obvious isn't always obvious. It depends on your focus.

Some folks blame everything on the devil and look for a demon under every rock. I joke about people who even bind the postnasal-drip demon. Satan is a real entity and I don't want to downplay his influence, but he shouldn't be the center of our focus.

When Jesus was in the wilderness, Satan misused Scripture three times in an attempt to trip up the Lord. But the Son of God had the right focus. He told His enemy straight out, "Get out of here, Satan. For the Scriptures say, 'You must worship the Lord your God; serve only him.'"[1] We cannot let Satan take our focus off God. If we do, we've missed the point.

–GC

Holy God, I don't want anything to take my focus off You. When Satan tempts me, help me to keep looking at You and not at the tempter or the temptation. I want to worship You and You alone. Amen.

TODAY'S READING: MATTHEW 4:1-11; REVELATION 19:6-10;
PSALMS 29:2; 95:6; 99:5; 99:9

The Rules of the Road

For you have been called to live in freedom—not freedom to satisfy your sinful nature, but freedom to serve one another in love.

GALATIANS 5:13

In racing, some rules are etched in stone. They don't change. Others, however, are open to interpretation. They change according to circumstances and the particular people involved.

Some rules are obvious: The size of the restrictor plate that regulates how much fuel goes in the carburetor is limited; the race-car's shape must fit into certain templates; the type of fuel is restricted; and the capacity of the gas tank is uniform. These rules are not open for discussion. If someone breaks them, that person is busted.

Other rules are more vague. When a rule is not precise, it leaves the door open for various interpretations. It's like telling a child, "Don't watch a movie on *that* TV." Then they watch a movie on a different TV and say, "Well, you said not to watch it on *that* TV. You didn't say I couldn't go into my bedroom and watch it on *my* TV." Racers are like kids. We live on the edge of the rules.

At the track, rules that are open to interpretation include speeds on pit road and the difference between aggressive driving and driving that is too aggressive. Determining what's intentional and what's not is always an issue. And now that bump-and-run has become the end-of-the-race move of choice, there is more pressure on the officials to interpret the rules.

Auto racing is like basketball. Some referees will call a foul every time someone touches an opposing player. Another ref will allow pushing and bumping. Professional basketball players have six fouls. Most guys spend two just to find out how the officials are going to call the game. It's the same with racing. We push the envelope to see how the rules will be enforced.

The rules do not apply the same to everybody. It's true in basketball, and it's true in racing. Rookies have to tow the mark much closer than veterans do. I got away with a ton when I was driving in the 1980s.

—DW

Some of God's rules are etched in stone, like the Ten Commandments. Murder, lying, stealing and worshiping idols are a few of the absolute no-nos.

Other rules are variables. They are open to interpretation, and they don't apply equally to everyone. Going to the movies, dancing, playing cards, gambling and drinking alcohol are just a few that are malleable. For some, they are sin, but for others they are not. Our ability to constantly hear and obey the Holy Spirit will determine the boundaries God has for each of us. Some variables will be sin for me, but won't be sin for my wife, and vice versa. If God convicts us about a certain act, we should not do it. If He doesn't, we can press on as long as we don't violate God's absolutes and don't cause others to stumble.[1]

When we try to make our boundaries someone else's boundaries, we become legalistic. If we flaunt our freedoms, we may cause others to disregard the boundaries God has for them. If they stumble or fall because of our carelessness, we have sinned, too.

Unlike the officials in NASCAR or basketball, God cuts rookies some slack, but He's real tough on veterans. Five times Moses made excuses to keep from having to go talk to the pharaoh, with no consequences. Then late in life, at his second rock-calling contest, He dishonored God in front of the people and had to go up on a mountain and die.[2] Now that is some consequence! Thankfully, He does not always do that.

In racing, hoops and life in general, we usually try to see how bad we can be and still get by. But if this is our attitude with God, we won't be OK, no matter what we do. He wants our hearts. Once we give it to Him, He will give us great freedom. We shouldn't take license with our liberties or kick against our boundaries. God wants us to enjoy freedom, but He doesn't want us to fall.

–JC

Dear loving God of grace and mercy, show me the freedom You have given to me and reveal my boundaries. I worship and honor You. I want to please You, through Jesus Christ, my Lord. Thank You.

TODAY'S READING: EXODUS 20:1-20; 31:18; MATTHEW 5:27-28;
1 CORINTHIANS 8:7-9; GALATIANS 5:13-14

Real Bad Rubbish

I consider everything a loss compared to the surpassing greatness of knowing Christ Jesus my Lord, for whose sake I have lost all things. I consider them rubbish, that I may gain Christ and be found in him, not having a righteousness of my own that comes from the law, but that which is through faith in Christ.

PHILIPPIANS 3:8-9, NIV

Before 1983, I didn't think much about bad language. I just used it all the time. After recommitting my life to Christ, I thought about it, but I didn't do much about it—especially on race day. Then I had children—that cleaned up my act around the house. Improper language is wrong, but I still had a problem at the track. At the end of my driving career, I was working hard on not cussing or swearing.

Now I'm in broadcasting. It bothers me a lot when a lack of language skills keeps me from getting my point across. I'm a good communicator, but now I can't use the same words. Being on TV every week, I must have a good grasp of the English language and be able to express myself in a way that's appealing to the viewers. The trash-talking that I've done my whole life in the garage, pits and car has limited me. I cannot talk trash in the booth.

This is one of my most troublesome areas. I know what the Bible declares about using bad language. Thankfully, I am at the point where I usually only cuss or swear when I'm angry. That's not an excuse. It's still wrong. It is just the truth.

When I was in a race car, only my crew chief could hear what I was saying. We frequently used every word I now cannot use on television. In 2004, I'll be talking to more than 17 million people each race day. It will not be like talking to my crew chief. I'll be using cleaner language to make my points.

There was a time when I was one of 43 voices on the track. Now, I am the voice! That just shows the power of TV. I have come to realize that with power comes responsibility. I know my sport. I can remember most of the facts without going to a cheat sheet. I also comprehend the issues. But I have to make sure I communicate properly—not just to keep my job, but because of whom I represent.

—DW

The apostle Paul was a tough guy. He took his lickings and kept on ticking. There wasn't a wishy-washy bone in his body. Paul was a good talker. He wasn't mistaken for Hermes, the god of oratory,[1] for no reason. His toughness occasionally came through in his speech, but he didn't cuss.

One time Paul was confronted with a proposition suggesting that Christians should sin more so that God would have more opportunities to demonstrate His grace. Translations of his response vary, but they are all firm: "God forbid." "May it never be." "Of course not."[2] Paul didn't use the four-letter h-word. Instead, he used the strongest words possible without crossing the line and swearing.

He used the same technique in his letter to the Philippians to communicate another concept. *The King James Version* used the word "dung."[3] In another verse, it means "manure" (as in fertilizer), but in our featured passage, "rubbish" means "refuse to be thrown to the dogs."

Paul's choice is a word of emphasis. It is a focused word. It includes anything that takes us away from the bull's-eye. It is a collective word, too. It rounds up everything extraneous, throws it onto one pile and gives it a label: dung. This, however, is not referring to excrement. It is neither the s nor the c word. Think *real bad rubbish* and you're close. Again, Paul used strong language, but he didn't cross the line.

Anything in our lives that interferes with growth in Jesus Christ is real bad rubbish. Anything that's more important to us than the Son of God belongs on the manure pile, and that includes the language we use.

There is a place for firm language, but there is no place for profanity or coarse talk. We need to keep working on our language, especially when we get mad, so that everything that comes out of our mouths will bring glory to God.[4] DW is working overtime to gain victory in this area of life. Are you?

–*GC*

Wonderful counselor, I want everything that comes out of my mouth to be
pleasing to You, especially when I get angry. I don't want to sin when
I'm upset. Starting today, I choose to give up those words that don't bring
glory to Your Name. May it be so.

TODAY'S READING: ROMANS 6:1-11; PHILIPPIANS 3:1-16;

MATTHEW 12:34; EPHESIANS 4:25-30

Payback

See that no one pays back evil for evil, but always try to do good to each other and to everyone else.

1 THESSALONIANS 5:15

You must make allowance for each other's faults and forgive the person who offends you. Remember, the Lord forgave you, so you must forgive others.

COLOSSIANS 3:13

Racing is supposed to be a chess match. It used to be a game of wit. It's not supposed to be about the bumper. The bumper is there to keep a driver from knocking his radiator in, not to use to get other drivers out of the way.

I always say a smart race-car driver does not have a scratch on his car at the end of the day. My goal, every time I drove a race at a half-mile track, like Martinsville or Bristol, where contact is expected, was to sit in Victory Circle with everybody else's car looking like it had been in a demolition derby and mine looking like it had just rolled off the showroom floor.

If I had to rough a guy up a little bit to get by him, the win didn't feel nearly as good as one that I won by outsmarting and outdriving the other drivers. It's a lot easier to hit a guy and knock him out of the way, but that is a cheap shot. A lot of boxers can knock out Mike Tyson if he doesn't know they are going to hit him.

Dale Earnhardt aggravated me. He would rather hit somebody than race around him. He had all the ability in the world. He could outdrive anybody. He didn't have to hit other cars, but he wanted to do it. He made rough driving popular. Fans used to boo it. Now they love it.

Dale liked that image of being the intimidator. When another driver saw him in his rearview mirror, Dale wanted that driver to move out of the way so that Dale would not hit him. Hitting Dale did not work. If a driver hit him once, he'd hit back twice. That was his philosophy. It was his payback.

—DW

This is a tough one. Whether it is in sports, business or the community, how should we treat people in a way that we want to be treated? How do we not bump them back twice when they have bumped us?

When I played basketball, if I knew my opponent was a dirty player, I made it a point to hit him first. That way we would at least be even by the end of the game, and I might be one up on him if I got in the last lick. But I didn't play that way against everybody. With the good guys, I just played hard. Of course, I wasn't trying to please God in those days.

The legendary coach John Wooden has an interesting take on this dilemma. When he coached at UCLA, winning was not his goal. Getting his players to perform at their best was what he sought, and he was willing to let winning take care of itself. He believes anything that diverts the players away from doing their best ought to be jettisoned.

We can't do our best at anything in life if we are thinking about getting even for some wrong. When we have a mind-set of revenge, we give our opponent the advantage.

In the spiritual realm, we need to understand our opponent. He is the devil and he is real. He hates God, and he hates us because God loves us. Satan doesn't want to spend eternity with us, but neither does He want us to spend eternity with God. To that end, he will do anything to take our eyes away from God.

Perhaps you are a victim of something awful: rape, alcoholism, divorce or domestic violence. Perhaps someone you trusted abused your child. Whatever the circumstances of the offense, you probably want revenge. You want payback. God sees it in a different way. He is the One who ultimately metes out justice. He only wants you to turn the person who did those awful things over to Him. To grant forgiveness is tough, but it takes away our opponent's advantage and gives the payback to God.

–GC

Gracious forgiver and protector of my soul, give me the courage to turn those who have harmed me and the ones I love over to You and Your discipline. Don't allow the adversary to gain the advantage. I want to keep my total focus on You. Thank You.

TODAY'S READING: ROMANS 12:17-21; HEBREWS 10:26-31; MATTHEW 5:38-47; EPHESIANS 4:26-27; 1 THESSALONIANS 5:15; COLOSSIANS 3:12-17

Eating Crow

But when you are praying, first forgive anyone you are holding a grudge against, so that your Father in heaven will forgive your sins, too.

MARK 11:25

We were racing at Rockingham in 1992. On the last lap of the race, I was running sixth and Ricky Craven was running seventh. We went into the third turn, and we were going toward the checkereds when Ricky drove underneath me and slammed me into the fence. He finished sixth and I finished wrecked. I was livid.

I hadn't healed from my real bad wreck, and I was still walking with a limp. Well, after the race, I took off. I looked like Old Chester, limp-hopping on one leg trying to chase Ricky down. I went to his car, jerked down his window net, grabbed him by the throat and started yelling. I didn't hit him, but I was up in his face, calling him everything you could call somebody. Here I was screaming and throwing a fit—and I was Ricky's hero. He looked up to me. I had even witnessed to him.

Finally, I let go of Ricky and returned to my hauler. The more I thought about what had happened, the madder I got. I started yelling, "I'm goin' back. I'm gonna knock his block off."

Well, about that time Max Helton walked up. He's the director of Motor Racing Outreach. He said, "Now, DW, you just need to calm down."

I said, "Max, get out of my way. I'm goin' down there and I'm goin' up in that boy's truck, and I'm gonna jack his jaw."

Max stood across the door, put his hands up and said, "Look, if you're that mad, just hit me. I'd rather you hit me than go down there and cause yourself problems. Come on. If it'll make you feel better and you gotta hit somebody, just hit me."

I cracked up. I said, "Max, come on. I can't hit you."

He said, "Well, you can't go down there and hit him either. You've just got to remember who you are."

A week later, we were in Phoenix for the next race. Max asked me to open the chapel service with prayer. Stevie and I were sitting in the front row. I stood up, walked to the podium, turned around, and guess who was sitting in the front row, looking me right in the eyes? Ricky Craven! I thought, *God, what are You doin'?*

It was one of those convicting moments. My first thought was *I'm just gonna bow my head, pray and press on.* But as I stood there, the Lord said, "Look, I don't want to hear a prayer from you. You've got business to take care of. You've got something you've got to straighten out before you talk to Me."

So I said, "Folks, I can't pray until I ask Ricky Craven to forgive me. Ricky, will you come up here, please?" So Ricky came up. I put my arm around him and said, "Man, I love you. I'm sorry about what happened last week. That was a big mistake. I hope you'll forgive me."

He said, "Man, I would forgive you. That's not a problem. Will you forgive me?"

I said, "Yes, I will." We hugged each other right there. Then he sat down, and I prayed.

—DW

Has someone wrecked you or someone you love? You're probably holding a grudge—we all do. The Bible shows us a better way: "If you forgive those who sin against you, your heavenly Father will forgive you."[1] This is an important verse, but we shouldn't misunderstand it. If we know Jesus personally, a failure to forgive someone won't keep us out of God's kingdom. Jesus died for all of our sins, both confessed and unconfessed. However, unconfessed sin will make us powerless.

For the believer, unconfessed sin grieves God and quenches the power of the Holy Spirit. Darrell knew his prayer would be worthless until he got right with Ricky. To his credit, he did, and God was well pleased.

Although it's no fun to eat crow, it's better than eating your own insides. Do you need to eat some crow to get right with God?

—JC

Holy counselor, bring to mind those whom I have wronged.
Give me the courage to ask their forgiveness. Bring to mind those
who have wronged me. I want to forgive them by giving up my desire
to get even and by turning them over to You and Your discipline.
I want to be right with You. Thank You, Lord.

TODAY'S READING: MATTHEW 6:14; 18:21-35; ACTS 7:54-60;
2 CORINTHIANS 2:5-11; MARK 11:25-26

Where They Are

But when some of the teachers of religious law who were Pharisees saw him eating with people like that, they said to his disciples, "Why does he eat with such scum?" When Jesus heard this, he told them, "Healthy people don't need a doctor—sick people do. I have come to call sinners, not those who think they are already good enough."

MARK 2:16-17

We were having a Bible study in a hotel meeting room in Martinsville. One of the crew members had come out of the bar and was heading to the bathroom, and he had a beer. His name was Earl, and he looked in and saw us. We all knew each other, so we said, "Hey, Earl. Whatcha doin'?"

Earl walked in and said, "Oh, I was just havin' a few cold ones. What y'all got goin' on in here?"

I said, "Well, we're havin' a little Bible study. Why don't you join us?"

"Well, um . . . you know, um," Earl hesitated. "What'll I do with my beer?"

Max was teaching and said, "Look, go get all your buddies and bring your beer in here if you want. We'd love to have you." So he did. Earl brought his beer and two other guys with their beers, and they came in, sat down and listened for a while. I loved that. We didn't make a big deal out of the beer. They were inquiring, and it was a start. Sometimes that's all a person needs.

Another time, we were at a Motor Racing Outreach conference in Orlando when a popular driver named Kenny was trying to figure out the faith. "You know, this is a hell of a lot harder than I thought," he said. "And there's a hell of a lot more to it than I thought there was, too." I loved that, too—not the language, but the honesty. We didn't make a big deal out of a couple swear words. For Kenny it was a start, and it was good.

It's one thing to have been in the faith for years and still act like a baby. But it's quite another to expect inquirers to act like mature believers. We weren't shocked by Earl's beer or Kenny's language. We just met them where they were.

It would be great to welcome them to the family, and I hope we gave them a good start.

–DW

What DW did with Earl and Kenny is exactly what Jesus did with the woman at the well.[1] Our Lord wasn't shocked when she spoke to Him, even though she was probably a prostitute. We know that, because in that culture any woman who would talk to a man on the street who was a stranger would have been a lady of the night. The woman at the well had lived with five guys in as many years, so if she wasn't a whore, she was at least a loose woman with a very bad reputation.

It is easy to understand why the disciples were mortified when they saw their leader talking with her. They were embarrassed and concerned— embarrassed by Jesus' behavior and concerned about all of their reputations. They hadn't yet learned the lesson. Jesus was trying to teach His followers to meet people where they were.

Not long before the meeting at the well, Jesus violated several Jewish rules to try to teach His men the same lesson. They all had dinner with tax gatherers and Gentiles.[2] In those days, a good Jewish person would not enter into a house where Gentiles were present, let alone eat and drink with them.

The people at this party were considered by the Pharisees to be "tax collectors and sinners."[3] The tax gatherers were usually Jewish, but other Jewish people would not associate with them. Tax collectors were the most hated individuals in Israel because they were locals who represented Rome and got rich by using Roman authority to collect more taxes than were due. They even pocketed the excess. In this setting, the only friends the Jewish tax collectors had were Gentiles—and according to the Jewish culture of the day, another word for Gentile was "sinner."

Jesus met people where they were. The result was a fresh start for both the woman at the well and a tax gatherer named Matthew, who would become one of the 12 disciples. Are you meeting people where they are? Who can you help get started in the faith?

–*gc*

Heavenly Father, help me to do away with any biases that may be in me. I want to be available to minister to anyone You place in my path. Help me to meet people where they are and use me to start others in the faith. Thank You, Lord.

TODAY'S READING: 1 PETER 3:13-17; MARK 2:13-17;
JOHN 4:5-42; MATTHEW 9:9-13

Slowing Down

But when the Holy Spirit controls our lives, he will produce this kind of fruit in us: love, joy, peace, patience, kindness, goodness, faithfulness, gentleness, and self-control. Here there is no conflict with the law.

GALATIANS 5:22-23

People going slow in the left lane of a freeway bug me. I'm a race-car driver. Don't be blocking me. Turn me loose. I mean, if you don't want me on your back bumper, get out of my lane. I know people look in the mirror and they see me behind them, and I know that their first thought is *I'm gonna slam on the brakes and "brake check" that dude.* But I know that is what they are thinking, so that's why I drive with both feet. Go ahead, sucker. I'm a race-car driver!

Some days when I get on the road, it's packed and I can't go anywhere—I'm in a box, stuck. I hate to be in a box. It's really difficult for me to creep along or have to wait.

This is true with everything I do: I'm always on a mission. That's just who I am. When the family is going somewhere, I get ready and then wait forever at the back door for the kids and Stevie. I can run out a tank of gas waiting. I'm very impatient, and I'm a perfectionist. Put those two characteristics together in one person, and it's enough to drive others crazy. Just ask my wife and kids.

But I'm managing stuff better than I ever have before. I'm not as antsy on the freeway. I'm not grousing as much while I'm waiting. I'm tempering my man-on-a-mission mind-set. I can handle things not going my way better than ever. It's a challenge though. I've challenged myself to be under more self-control and to let God demonstrate the fruit of the Holy Spirit in my life.

I choose one challenge a week. One week I will work on love: showing love to others and being a loving, caring family. Another week, I will work on self-control. This means that when I am on the freeway, I need to work on being patient.

It's slow going. I'm such a piece of work. But I really do want to look more and more like Jesus.

–DW

I'm on Maui, sitting in a studio apartment writing this book. I have to stay here a whole month. The blues of the sky and the sea clash, and the fluffy white clouds drifting by create these ugly contrasts on the surface of the shimmering water. An island spoils the view of the horizon and the trade winds make the palm trees sway in a way that is quite distracting. The waves and the birds make an awful lot of noise. Sounds grim, doesn't it? This is killing me.

When the planes land, all the people from the mainland hurry to their rental cars, hotels, beaches, dinners and shows. It takes a few days for them to adjust. My favorite bumper sticker adorns many cars on Maui: "Slow down, this ain't the mainland." DW would probably go crazy here. Either that, or he'd make everybody else crazy. Whichever way, he would get to work a lot on that challenge of being more patient.

There is an old saying, "I want patience, and I want it right now!" Patience is a biggie. We all need more, and we need it yesterday.

God has a lot to say about patience. The book of Ephesians has a list of good stuff that God gives us. Right there in the middle of what is called the fruit of the Spirit is patience. The others are love, joy, peace, kindness, goodness, faithfulness, gentleness and self-control. Together they define what love is. When they are being demonstrated in my life, then I am demonstrating love. And one of the biggies is patience.

The book of James also brings home the importance of patience. It uses the word "endurance," but it means the same thing. "Let endurance have its perfect result, so that you may be perfect and complete, lacking in nothing."[1] None of the other components packs the punch of being perfect and complete, lacking in nothing. When we practice patience, we've mastered the biggest part of what it means to love. And when we show more love, we look more like Jesus.

–GC

Dear Lord God, I'm almost afraid to ask for patience and the ability to endure. Those lessons tend to come with pain. Father, please fill me so full of Your Spirit that I won't know I'm being cooked. Thank You.

TODAY'S READING: GALATIANS 5:16-24; JAMES 1:2-8; 1 PETER 5:6-11

Taking the Next Step

I don't mean to say that I have already achieved these things or that I have already reached perfection! But I keep working toward that day when I will finally be all that Christ Jesus saved me for and wants me to be.

PHILIPPIANS 3:12

Because of who I am and what I've done, I have a unique platform. People are always looking for a personality to speak at events and gatherings. Organizers prefer speakers who can make people laugh. I can do that. I'm a good storyteller, too. I've got a story for everything. I like to make people laugh, but I really like telling them how I've been affected by God. I talk about what God has done in my heart, in my marriage and in all areas of my life.

I think people accept my style—they know that I'm not a preacher. I'm a race-car driver who can be entertaining, but God is working on me. He has shown me that I don't know His Word well enough to represent Him like I should in a broader range of venues. I'm great at a banquet. I need to be better at church.

Being a good storyteller is not a good excuse for not knowing God's Word. I need to do a better job of studying and preparing before I speak. I need to know more about what God wants me to talk about. My lack of knowledge is my own fault because I have a good memory. I can listen to a song a couple of times, then go out and sing every word. I can tell you what springs I ran in my car at Darlington in 1972. But I have a hard time quoting Scripture. It's not because I can't. It's just because I haven't.

That's where I am with God right now. God is showing me how much more I need to know. I can't preach the Word if I don't know it. I can't say the right things if I don't know what I'm talking about. I can't converse with someone about salvation, grace or other spiritual matters unless I really know what the Bible declares. That is one place where God is still working on me.

Since I made my recommitment to Christ, life has been a journey of obedience. He has been faithful in directing me. Learning more about His Word and working it into my speaking are what He has decided I should work on next.

–DW

The moment had come to get His men ready. Jesus would die soon and there was little time left to give directions, so He took the disciples to Caesarea Philippi. At the time, it was the center of supernatural activity.

At the base of Mount Hermon there is a cave, and during the times when people worshiped Baal and Pan, 25 percent of the Jordan River flowed out of it. In those days, people believed the fertility gods lived in the cave. Worshipers threw human sacrifices in the cave opening to try to please their gods.

Imagine Jesus with His disciples standing before a huge rock. An opulent Roman temple rises to the right. Each of five indentations in the stone holds a statue of Pan. The cavelike opening to the left is called the Gates of Hell. It is in that setting that Jesus asks the most important question ever asked: "Who do you say that I am?"[1]

It was loudmouthed Peter who got it right: "You are the Messiah, the Son of the living God."[2]

Jesus then said that He would build His church on "this rock" and that the "powers of hell" will not overpower it.[3] The rock Jesus refers to is the confession that Jesus is the Christ, the Son of the living God.

The temple represented the most powerful empire the world had ever seen and all the empires that would follow. Jesus said that the Roman Empire and all the rest wouldn't prevail. The five false idols and the Baals that preceded them represented all the idols the world had or would ever offer. Jesus said they wouldn't stand. The cave represented the very gates of hell. And Jesus said Satan doesn't stand a chance. Not empires, not false gods, not even the devil himself can overpower the confession that Jesus Christ is Lord. Upon that Rock, you can rest assured.

A correct answer to the most important question ever asked is the starting point. Who do you say that Jesus is? If your answer is, "He is the Christ, the Son of the living God," then, just as God has done with DW, He will also start working on you. He'll decide what you are to work on next.

–GC

Holy teacher, I confess Jesus is the Christ. He is Your Son. Thank You for Him. Don't allow me to become complacent with my faith or satisfied with my relationship with You. I want to keep on growing in You. Show me what is next. Thank You.

TODAY'S READING: MATTHEW 16:13-20; EPHESIANS 2:13-22; PHILIPPIANS 3:1—4:1

Bigger Plans

"For I know the plans I have for you," says the LORD. "They are plans for good and not for disaster, to give you a future and a hope. In those days when you pray, I will listen. If you look for me in earnest, you will find me when you seek me."

JEREMIAH 29:11-13

Fox Sports broadcasts the first half of the NASCAR season. NBC airs the second half. NBC doesn't have football. Fox does. Fox couldn't do the entire year because its production people do both auto racing and football.

Fox airs 18 races. NFL football has 17 weeks of games, not counting the preseason and postseason. That means that John Madden and I work about the same number of weeks per year.

God put me in a perfect situation. I get to go to the races, keep my airplane and keep my motor coach. At the racetrack, I'm treated like I'm still driving. I get to enjoy everything that I loved about the sport, but without the headaches or the risk. I don't have to worry about how my car is going to run. I no longer care how the cars run on Sunday, except maybe my brother Michael's. I just hope they run so that I can talk about them.

When I was driving, I had a core group of fans who cheered for me every week. Those fans followed me when I went into the television broadcast booth, but I have so many more fans now. When I say something nice about Tony Stewart, his fans like me. When I compliment Dale Earnhardt, Jr., or Jeff Gordon, I pick up some more fans, and more fans mean more influence for the Kingdom. I have to tell you, I love the plans God has had for me.

I was talking with my mom about racing. I said something about how hard I've worked over the years, and she looked at me and said, "Son, you never worked a day in your life." She was right. I've been blessed beyond belief. I have been able to earn a living doing something I thoroughly love. I guess it doesn't look like work when you love it.

—DW

I had been a traveling preacher for 25 years. I loved being up front, and I thoroughly enjoyed taking an audience through both laughter and tears to a point of commitment. Speaking was my ministry, vocation, hobby, livelihood and identity. But it came to a halt on May 21, 2002.

That Tuesday evening, while I was delivering the last message of my three-day series, my voice began to crack and fluctuate, and my throat hurt. My voice quality was gone, and I could no longer project without pain.

When I returned home, I went to a throat doctor and discovered that I had a paralyzed vocal cord on the right side. I tried a variety of ministries while I waited on the Lord—none of them was fulfilling. I finally got to the point where I said, "Lord, I'm 62, and I've tried everything I can think of, and I'm out of options. If You want me on the shelf, I'll go on the shelf. If my influence for the Kingdom is done, then that's Your call, and I'll be OK with it. I will now rest in You."

Two days later, I got a call from a friend who suggested that I go see Coach John Wooden. I had always wanted to have breakfast with my basketball mentor. I was on my way home from breakfast when I got an idea I believe was from God. Coach thought it was a good one, too, and we wrote *Coach Wooden One-on-One. Darrell Waltrip One-on-One* is the second in the series. With these two books, I will "talk" to twice as many people as I have in 25 years of public speaking.

A previous reading noted that it took DW 10 years to come to the end of himself. It only took me a year. But when we finally gave up our plans, God executed His plans. Giving up gets results, because God's plans are best. Who would have guessed that God's plans included exponentially expanded influence for the Kingdom for a couple of old geezers who just want to serve God? Now DW's got more fans and I've got more readers. Isn't that great? It sure doesn't feel like work when you're having this much fun.

Are you operating under your plans or His? His are more fun.

–GC

Oh, great God of eternal wonder, thank You for the plans You have for me.
Thank You for bringing me to the end of myself, and
thank You for being there for me in ways I never imagined.
Father God, I am grateful. Thank You.

TODAY'S READING: PSALMS 33:11; 40:5; ISAIAH 14:24; 55:9;
2 CORINTHIANS 4:15; JEREMIAH 29:11-13

Mondays

Since everything around us is going to melt away, what holy, godly lives you
should be living! You should look forward to that day and hurry it along—
the day when God will set the heavens on fire and the elements will melt
away in the flames. But we are looking forward to the new heavens and
new earth he has promised, a world where everyone is right with God.
And so, dear friends, while you are waiting for these things to happen, make
every effort to live a pure and blameless life. And be at peace with God.

2 PETER 3:11-14

I am like a pastor. I have to work on Sunday. Many pastors take Monday
off. Not me. I can't. That is my day to put out fires. If it rains on my parade,
it will rain on a Monday.

How I feel on a Monday depends on my performance on Sunday. If I did
well the day before, it makes Monday a great day to be alive. If I didn't, I
want to crawl under a rock. This was true when I raced, and it is true now
that I am in the broadcast booth.

Monday is when I open mail. Often there's stuff I do not want to see. There
are phone calls, too. During racing season, I am at the track Thursday through
Sunday. Friends call me on Monday morning to tell me how I did. Sometimes
they liked my analysis; other times they didn't. Everyone has an opinion.

When I was racing, if I had a great Sunday, on Monday people could
toss all the curves they wanted at me. I was ready for anything. When I had
won, I felt that I could walk on water. I would wake up thinking, *Come on,*
day, bring it on. I'm ready for whatever you've got to throw at me.

As my racing career wound down, almost weekly I suffered through the
burden of not doing well, of not winning, of not performing. I no longer
had what it took to get the job done. The pressure was intense. It was just
like being the quarterback of a football team: When the team loses, it is
always the quarterback's fault. In NASCAR, it is always the driver's fault.

The blame came with the territory, but it still would get me down. I
could handle a little adversity because that was part of being a driver, but
I just couldn't handle it every week, especially not every week for several
years. At the end, it seemed like every day was a Monday after a bad race.

—DW

I am a traveling preacher. When I speak at a camp or conference center on a weekend, I take Monday off. Like a race-car driver, I tend to let how I perform at a certain meeting affect me. I shouldn't, but I do. Also, people like to analyze my illustrations, my points and my altar call. I let that affect me, too. I shouldn't, but I do.

I remember one night when about 50 kids decided to rededicate their lives to Christ, 3 people received Jesus as their Savior and around 15 made sure that their previous decisions to serve the Lord were real. The night before, more than 40 kids had accepted Christ. For a preacher like me, this was like how winning the Daytona 500 was for DW, only with results that boomerang through eternity.

I was dazzled. God solved the problem of eternity for a bunch of kids, even though sometimes I still wonder what that really means. I confess that I do not have much of a grasp on the magnitude of God's ways. Eternity is too big of a concept for my puny mind. I only know that God did something amazing through this old jock. I love being used by Him and being a part of eternal things, even if I do not see the entire picture. It adds so much meaning to my life.

I know that my job is to tell the story and to leave the results to God. To that end, how I perform has nothing at all to do with what the Holy Spirit does or doesn't do. And I know that all God wants from me is to worship Him and to be obedient. Just the same, when a meeting goes well and when the harvest is great, it makes Monday a very good day. When it goes awry, I just want to sleep in on Monday.

What happened yesterday shouldn't affect today. The trick is to not let our circumstances affect our relationship with God or with others. As we mature in Christ, we should become so close to the Father that what's going on around us won't change a thing. Besides, when we are always looking back at Sunday, we risk missing what Monday might bring.

–*JC*

Almighty Father in heaven, help me to be so focused on You that my Christian walk will be consistent, regardless of what's going on around me. Give me the strength to be a constant mirror of Christ who lives in me. Thank You.

TODAY'S READING: 2 CORINTHIANS 6:1-11; JAMES 3:13-18; 2 PETER 3:8-13

The Big Red Truck

I saw the dead, both great and small, standing before God's throne. And the books were opened, including the Book of Life. And the dead were judged according to the things written in the books, according to what they had done.

REVELATION 20:12

In NASCAR, we have a Big Red Truck. It's where drivers go when they've messed up. A summons to the Big Red Truck is like a summons to court and a sentence to jail at the same time. I have been in the Big Red Truck many times as a driver, and I've been inside once as an announcer.

On race day, when you get to the gate and when you move from one area to another, weekend officials check the hard card, or pass, around your neck to make sure you're where you're supposed to be. The officials all know me, so if they stop me, it's because they want to talk or they just want to mess with me.

I was at Dover, where there is no tunnel under the track to the infield. Smitty, who drives my motor coach, and I were in the infield in our golf cart and it had been raining. To get across the track, we had to go to the front straightaway, which has gates on both sides. The television booth was on the outside, and I was in a hurry because I thought we were about to go on the air. Because of the rain, the practice schedule for the drivers had been changed, but I didn't know it.

As we got to the crossing gate, the officials motioned for us to stop. I thought all they wanted to do was talk, so I told Smitty to keep going. We got out on the track and saw the race cars. The scene looked like a speeding locomotive bearing down on a car trying to cross the tracks. We got out of the way in time, but almost crossing in front of the speeding race cars gave us a rush.

John Darby summoned us to the Big Red Truck. We didn't know how bad we were busted. If I lost the cart and my hard card, I would not be able to do my job. As it turned out, Darby was a nice guy, and he accepted our explanation. He just chewed on us a little, and then he let me go back to work.

The Big Red Truck is kind of like the Great White Throne of Judgment. Drivers and, in this case, one announcer, go in there on their knees, because whatever Darby decides is final.

–DW

NASCAR has its Big Red Truck, but we can find thrones of judgment everywhere if we look.

Did you ever get called to the principal's office when you were a kid? Shooting spit wads seems pretty piddly these days, but it was big enough to have to go and see the Man when I was a kid. The wait before being called in was the worst. I got suspended for a day.

In another incident, I was locked off base for a week. The high school I went to was on a United States Navy base. I lived off the base, but my girl-friend lived inside. I needed a pass to get through the gate. Those who lived inside had "XTC" on their passes, which gave them exchange, theater and commissary privileges. Since I wanted to go to the movies with my girl-friend, I altered my pass but got caught. I had to go see the big cheese who doled out the penalty. It was something like going to the Big Red Truck.

Then there was the time I got audited by the IRS. Getting everything ready and waiting for the knock on the door is a sobering time. Those guys have a lot of power, and they make you sweat. I had to borrow $14,000 to pay for the mistake my accountant had made.

All of the above experiences are mere child's play when compared to the Great White Throne of Judgment. Suspensions, lockouts, fines and back taxes are trivial compared to the consequences handed down at the ultimate judgment.

After the rapture occurs (the event Jerry Jenkins and Tim LaHaye made popular reading in their best-selling Left Behind series) and a series of end-time events unfold, including the final judgment of unbelievers, the Book of Life and books of records will be opened.[1] Only those who have trusted Jesus Christ as Savior will have their names recorded in the Book of Life. The names of those who have rejected Him won't be there. Their names will be in another book and their deeds will determine the severity of their pun-ishment. The good news is that if we know Jesus Christ, we never have to worry about the Great White Throne of Judgment.

–GC

Dear Father God, I chose to trust Jesus Christ with my soul. Thank You that He took my judgment upon His shoulders and that by trusting Him my name is in the Book of Life. Thank You that I don't have to appear before the Great White Throne of Judgment. Thank You.

TODAY'S READING: REVELATION 20:11-15; 1 THESSALONIANS 4:13–5:11; PSALM 62:12; JEREMIAH 17:10; MATTHEW 16:27

The Aha Experience

Oh, what joy for those whose disobedience is forgiven, whose sins are put out of sight. Yes, what joy for those whose sin is no longer counted against them by the Lord.

ROMANS 4:7-8

It took me a while, but I finally got it. It's one of the most difficult things that I had to come to terms with as a Christian. I did stuff that was against God's will, stuff that was offensive to God: sin. Some of my sins were worse than others but God hated them all. I had to confess them. Then He wiped the slate clean, but it took a while for me to believe that the slate was clean.

I knew He would wipe the slate clean, but I thought of it more like writing something on a piece of paper and then erasing it. The words have been erased, but there's still an image. If you hold the paper up to the light just right, you can still see the letters. That's how I felt. I thought, *OK, it's not there anymore; but if I turn it just right, I can see where it used to be.*

It's hard to accept the fact that the slate is clean. No image remains. A lot of people can't get over the stuff they've done. They live in the past. They won't accept total forgiveness and move on into the future. They do not fully understand how God treats confession.

I know I've done some terrible things in my past. But I have confessed them to God and I've confessed in front of my Christian friends. I've asked for forgiveness. God said, "You've got to tell your wife." So I did. There are things that I've done that I've told Stevie about. I hated to do it, but I had to do it so that she could forgive me.

I know God forgives. The Bible shows us that He does. That means that I can have a clear conscience about where I am today, even though it's hard to get there. It is hard because it is natural to think we can never be forgiven for things that we've done.

Christ died so that we could be forgiven of our sins. We've got to realize that, and we've got to take advantage of it.

–DW

Look at the following letters and determine which letter should follow N:

OTTFFSSEN

It could be an O since that's the letter starting the sequence. Perhaps it's an N since there is a single letter O preceding the double T. It could be a D spelling out the word "end" and putting an end to the string of letters. All are logical—but wrong. The missing letter is a T.

At this point, you know it is a T because I revealed it to you, but you don't know why. You probably aren't very excited. But when you know exactly how it fits, you will hardly be able to wait to show these letters to your friends. I have given you head knowledge, but if you aren't intimate with the letter, you're not very excited. Your excitement level is dependent on your relationship with the letter T, because the person who knows why it's the letter T has a different understanding. It's the same with Jesus Christ.

Most people in the United States are aware that Jesus claims to be the Son of God and the Savior of humankind. But as with the T, only those who are intimately acquainted are excited. Knowing about Jesus doesn't excite, but knowing Him is very exciting indeed.

Let me help you come into an intimate relationship with the letter T, at least in this sequence. Look at the letters, and then repeat the following words out loud: "one," "two," "three," "four," "five," "six," "seven," "eight," "nine" and "ten." Did you have an aha experience?

Most people have it by now, but just in case you don't, what are the first letters of each of the words for the numbers one through ten? The letter T represents the word "ten."

At the point you understood, you became intimate with the letter T and saw how the pieces fit together.

Like the old Darrell, there are lots of Christians who walk around not really believing that they have been totally forgiven. And there are plenty of people who don't believe in Jesus, who aren't concerned about forgiveness at all. DW finally had an aha experience with Jesus Christ and the concept of the forgiveness of sin. Have you?

–*JC*

Forgiving God in heaven, I confess that I am a sinner. Help me to understand forgiveness. I want to know Jesus Christ in a fresh, new way. I want to grow in Him and walk closer with Him. Lord, draw me near. Amen.

TODAY'S READING: PSALM 65:3; ROMANS 4:7-8; HEBREWS 8:12; EPHESIANS 1:7-14

This Bud's for God

For if you confess with your mouth that Jesus is Lord and believe in your
heart that God raised him from the dead, you will be saved. For it is
by believing in your heart that you are made right with God, and it is by
confessing with your mouth that you are saved.

ROMANS 10:9-10

I met Uncle Bud in Nantucket. As Stevie and I drove up to his house, we heard a loud, screaming voice. Uncle Bud did not know me from Adam, but he yelled, "Get under here!" Then he started cussing like a sailor. He was beneath the house fixing the plumbing and wanted help. That is Stevie's Uncle Bud.

Bud lost his wife in 2001. Stevie and the girls went to Aunt Limette's funeral. Uncle Bud had seen us having devotions as a family during our visits over the years and I had talked to him about the Lord, so he knew where we stood. Stevie is best at telling the rest of the story.

Bud was devastated. The morning after the service, he was crying and lamenting, "I'm never going to see her again. I've got to see her again. Do you think I'll see her again?" Such desperation. I told him that the only way for sure was if he went to heaven. I started at the beginning with creation and told him the whole story. Uncle Bud is 78 and acutely smart, but he's not a soft man. He's not an easy man to talk to. When I finished I said, "Uncle Bud, Jesus is holding out His hand, and He has the gift of forgiveness and eternal life for you."

Bud took my hand in his, and he said, "I want that gift." Then he laid his head on his arms across my knees, and we prayed. Uncle Bud received Christ.

Aunt Limette wanted to be cremated and have her ashes scattered on the beach. So a little later in the morning we went out to fulfill her wishes. We grouped together in a circle and Uncle Bud wanted to pray. He first asked his two grown children to forgive him for how unapproachable he had been his whole life. There were tears all around, and reconciliation took place in his family. It was the most incredible, instantaneous transformation I've ever seen.

–DW

Although it was late in his life, Stevie's Uncle Bud took a chance. Some call it a decision, but basically it was a bet. Uncle Bud bet his soul.

There is a rule in both gambling and business: Always weigh upside potential against downside risk. A buck isn't much. It doesn't matter much if you lose it. A life is worth a lot more. Proceed cautiously. Wagering a soul is the ultimate gamble. Be absolutely sure.

How good is your information regarding eternity? Is your source more reliable than the Bible? The 66 books of the Bible were written by 40 authors, including two kings, two priests, a physician, two fishermen, two shepherds, a legalistic theologian, a statesman, a tax collector, a soldier, a scribe, a butler and 25 others from equally diverse backgrounds, ranging from peasants and poets to statesmen and scholars. They wrote in the wilderness, dungeons, palaces, exile, times of war and times of peace, over a period of 1,600 years, in several countries, on three continents, in three languages and on hundreds of controversial subjects.

Even with all of these variables, this Book of books is in perfect harmony with itself and remains in precise agreement with all other factual, historical, archaeological and scientific works, both current and past. For example, while I believe that the parting of the Red Sea was miraculous, Russian scientists calculate that it was mathematically possible.[1]

The Bible contains flashes of inspired poetry as well as detailed history, captivating biographies, letters, memoirs and prophetic writings—yet it delivers astonishing continuity, miraculous accuracy and one unfolding story: God's redemption of men and women.

The harmony of the variables goes beyond the realm of chance. The Holy Bible is a miracle of God's preservation that can't be denied. The odds on the Bible's being wrong are a real long shot.

God said Jesus Christ is the only way to God the Father. Anyone who disagrees actually is attempting to make himself or herself God. That's a big mistake. Are you going to bet on Jesus or against Him?

Stevie dealt Uncle Bud the cards so that he could make a wager. Uncle Bud was 78 when he pushed all his chips into the center of the table and went all in. It's never too late to put your trust in Jesus Christ. Do you know anyone who needs to know what is in the Bible, so they can make their bet?

–*GC*

God in heaven, I choose redemption and forgiveness through Jesus Christ my Lord. I place my trust in Him. Amen.

TODAY'S READING: ROMANS 10:8-15; MATTHEW 10:24-33;
PHILIPPIANS 2:1-11; 1 JOHN 2:21-25

A Special Gift

I have fought a good fight, I have finished the race, and I have remained faithful. And now the prize awaits me—the crown of righteousness that the Lord, the righteous Judge, will give me on that great day of his return. And the prize is not just for me but for all who eagerly look forward to his glorious return.

2 TIMOTHY 4:7-8

Lord, just let me live long enough and be healthy enough to enjoy my grandchildren." These days I find myself saying this prayer often. Stevie and I are older parents. I'm 56, and Stevie is younger. Our daughters are 16 and 12 at the time of this writing. I hope Jessica (our oldest) doesn't get married when she's 18, but she could. I could be a grandfather in the next 5 to 10 years. It's probably going to be more like 10. I would not be that old—I would be 66, but that would be 76 when the first one would be 10 and 86 when he or she would be off to college.

I would like to be able to enjoy my grandchildren. And I'd like for them to be able to enjoy me. I didn't get much time with my grandfather on my dad's side. He died when I was a little boy. I didn't know him very well. I called my dad's mom Mamaw. My Mamaw Waltrip was older and a little frail, but I spent a lot of time with her. I stayed with her often because she was a widower and lived by herself. I kept her company—I liked doing that.

I knew my mom's mother and dad, Granny and Pappy, very well. Granny and Pappy took me to the races when I was a boy. When I got older and was competing in the races, they came to Nashville for the Winston Cup competition, held every year on the Saturday night before Mother's Day—I won that race a number of times. After the race, we would all go to the park and celebrate Mother's Day. They got to see my dreams come true, and that meant a lot to me.

I'd like to be able to have the same satisfaction with my grandchildren. How great it would be to take them to the Dairy Queen, ride around in a convertible and have them think that their grandpa was a cool old dude. I also would like to show them how to be faithful to God, even when I am old. I hope this is possible. That would be a special gift.

—DW

DW is heading toward old; I am a few years ahead of him. I already get to enjoy my grandchildren and sometimes they think I am cool. At my age, I also get to "enjoy" another "privilege": I have a bad back.

My back had gone out, so I checked myself into the hospital. Bill was my roommate. He was 87, had some dementia, several infected bedsores and bad bowels. It was tough being there. Three times during the night, Bill began to call for help. To my surprise, Scripture after Scripture tumbled out of his mouth, too.

The next day, as I was gathering my things, Bill's family arrived to see him. I asked, "Is Bill a Christian?"

"Oh, yes, but cataracts have kept him from reading his Bible," his son said.

At that moment Bill yelled at me: "Sonny, come over here and put my glasses on me. I want to see what you look like." As I did, he spoke again, "Thanks for helping me last night."

"Bill," I said, "You helped me far more than I helped you."

"How's that?" he asked, somewhat surprised.

I explained: "You showed me that it's possible to get so full of the Word of God that when all controls are turned off, the Word of God in a man's life can still overcome his sin nature."

Bill smiled and gave me a nod. I smiled back and nodded in response. It's the look two men share when each highly regards the other. As they wheeled him out for tests, I hollered, "Bill, I'll see you here, there or in the air."

The old man yelled from the hallway, "I'll be there. You can count on it!"

When I get as old as Bill, I want to be able to be like him. No, I'm not looking forward to dementia, bedsores or waiting for someone to come change my diaper. But I would love to be so full of the Word of God and so filled with the Holy Spirit that if all my physical and emotional control mechanisms were turned off, holiness would still come out. That would be a special gift. I met Bill, so I know it's possible.

–GC

Lord God, with all my heart I want to honor You with the rest of my life and represent You well to the people I love. Amen.

TODAY'S READING: 2 TIMOTHY 3:16—4:8; ACTS 20:24-27; REVELATION 21:6-8

All About Him

God can do anything, you know—far more than you could ever imagine or guess or request in your wildest dreams! He does it not by pushing us around but by working within us, his Spirit deeply and gently within us.

EPHESIANS 3:20, *THE MESSAGE*

Ever since I was 12 years old, I got up on Sunday, went to a track of some kind, put on a helmet, got behind a wheel of some type and raced. I did this for 41 years. When it was time to quit, I had this huge fear that I would lose my identity. I confess, I like driving down the highway and having people look over and yell, "Hey, there's DW. Boogity, boogity, boogity!"

When I would think about not racing, a chill would race through my spine. I had no idea how I could go on without racing. That was one of the reasons I hung on. I didn't want to have to face leaving. It got to the point where I didn't care whether I was starting on the pole or dead last. There's a good feeling about walking out onto the track on Sunday morning, walking down pit road, getting introduced to the crowd, hearing them cheer and then getting into your car.

The last few years of racing were the darkest of my life. It was a long, hard time. But it took the hard times to get me to gradually stop praying about me and start praying "Thy will be done." I quit whining "God, I don't want to stop racing," and I started asking, "Father, how can I best serve You?"

I'd never imagined that God could have something so much better for me. Broadcasting is the perfect spot at this stage of my life and career. It couldn't be a better fit for a show-off who likes to shoot off his mouth. It keeps me in the sport I love.

God had the perfect position waiting for me. He went beyond my wildest dreams, but I had to get my eyes off me and onto Him before it could happen.

—DW

A dog says: "You pet me, you feed me, you shelter me, you love me, you must be God."

A cat says: "You pet me, you feed me, you shelter me, you love me, I must be God."[1]

Bob Sjogren is the founder of Unveiling Glory, and he coined dog-and-cat theology. I love concept teaching, and this is a great example—if a person understands the differences between dogs and cats. I've had both. I understand.

Dogs have masters. Cats have servants. With a dog, it's all about you. With a cat, it's all about me (the cat).

We usually come to God in some kind of trouble as cats with a "God, help me" or "God, I don't want to go to hell" prayer. That's cat praying in its purest form. As new Christians we still do "Bail me out, God" prayers, but we expand them to include "I need this," "I want that," "Give it to me, God" and by the way, "Bless so-and-so." It's still mostly cat praying.

As we mature, our prayers should become more about God than ourselves. "Your Kingdom come," "What will bring glory to You?" and "What do You want me to do?" is the way our prayers ought to sound. We should also be praying more for other people than for ourselves. When we do this we are dog praying.

During DW's dark time, he started tithing around 15 percent of his income, not because he had to or felt pressure to do so, but because he wanted to. Stevie and DW helped start Motor Racing Outreach as a ministry to NASCAR families. He stopped taking chances on the racetrack for the sake of his family. And he started a Bible study in his garage. He changed.

It was during the dark time that DW's prayers and his behavior transformed from cat to dog. And when that happened, God dramatically expanded his influence.

We can trust a good old faithful pooch. But we just never know what a cat will do. Cats reflect themselves. Dogs reflect God. Are you a pooch yet?

–*JC*

Almighty God and protector of our souls, thank You that You don't let go of me, even when I let go of You. Thank You for patiently leading me to obedience. And thank You that Your plans go beyond my wildest dreams. Help me to be all about You, not me. May I be a mirror of Your glory today. Amen.

TODAY'S READING: EPHESIANS 3:20-21; JEREMIAH 29:11-14; EPHESIANS 1:1-14

Fast friends. For DW and Dale Earnhardt, Sr., what once was a bitter rivalry became a close camaraderie. Trackside, Dale, Sr., visits with the Waltrips (below). Before the 2004 Daytona 500, DW interviews Dale, Jr. (above).

The boogity, boogity, boogity goes on.
Although DW has retired as a NASCAR
driver, he is still a presence on the racing
scene. In Bristol, the grandstand was
named after him (above). Mentoring
younger drivers, DW cheers on David
Reutimann (right). And he competes
sometimes in the Craftsman Truck
series, driving the fabled number 17
(below, making a pit stop).

The Prayers of Many

I also tell you this: If two of you agree down here on earth concerning anything you ask, my Father in heaven will do it for you. For where two or three gather together because they are mine, I am there among them.

MATTHEW 18:19-20

Bill France, Sr., founded NASCAR. Once he was asked to give a prayer before a race. I'm guessing that he didn't do a lot of praying in public, at least not out loud. His prayer was short and simple: "Lord, bless the drivers. Lord, thank You for this great day." He closed with "Sincerely, Bill France." What was great is that he was sincere.

I do not like it when Christians use spiritual clichés and buzzwords in their prayers. I'm not into the old *King James* thees and thous either. Give me a good old, off-the-cuff, from-the-heart prayer any day.

The prayer I use the most is "God help me!" The Lord knows how often I need to get bailed out of the stuff I get myself into. But my two favorite prayers are the prayer of Jabez and the Lord's Prayer.

I never knew about the Jabez prayer until it became popular. Bruce Wilkinson made that a big deal. People love that prayer: "Bless me. Put Your hand on me. Enlarge my borders. Keep me free from fear and harm." Who wouldn't love that?

The prayer of Jabez is all about me, but the Lord's Prayer goes much further. Some of the Lord's Prayer is about me, but mostly it's about God: "Great is Your name. Bring Your kingdom. Your will be done." It is all focused on God's kingdom, God's power and God's glory. Since Jesus said to pray it, it must be the most important kind of prayer. Besides, prayer should be more about God than about me.

I made a huge discovery about prayer as I watched people pray at the men's Bible study I host in my garage each week. When we pray together—thus combining our prayers—something powerful happens. It doesn't seem to matter who prays or how they pray, but that we pray. When we are all in prayer, a lot of work seems to get done. I've seen many obviously answered prayers get checked off our Bible study prayer list. Praying as a group seems to make all the difference.

—DW

In 30 years of saying prayers, I have often seen the same difference that DW has seen: the more people praying, the greater the impact. Sometimes God answers with fireworks; other times He quietly meets an inner need.

At the height of communist persecution of Christians, God gave many extraordinary responses to prayer. Ioan Teodosiu, a young believer from the town of Sighisoara in Romania, saw one of them firsthand. He had been arrested, jailed and called an enemy of the state. A trial date was set, but the verdict of guilty was presumed and the penalty was to be death. His crime? Ioan helped put together an international prayer network for the persecuted Christians of his homeland. He also distributed Bibles brought in by Open Doors, Underground Evangelism and others—terrible blunders in a communist nation.

Just days before the trial, Ioan's wife, Ligia, was in tears, telling an American Christian friend that prayer was the only way out of the mess. Word went out. On the eve of the trial, members of John MacArthur's Grace Community Church in Panorama City, California, interceded for Ioan. So did Christians at nearby Church On The Way and hundreds of others around the world. Baptists, Pentecostals, Methodists, Lutherans—their theological differences did not matter; they united in prayer for Ioan.

On the day the trial was to be held, the American friend placed an international phone call to Ligia and actually got through. "Ioan is here. He is free," she almost shouted, juggling tears of relief and overwhelming joy. The friend would later learn that when it had been time for Ioan's trial to start, he was summoned into the office of one of the most prominent jurists in the nation. The communist powerbroker offered Ioan a seat and a cup of coffee. He even tasted the coffee first to show that it had not been poisoned. "I do not know why I am doing this," the jurist said, handing Ioan a train ticket back to Sighisoara. "Go home to your wife." Ioan was free indeed.[1]

God's answers are not always this dramatic, and His responses are not necessarily going to be what we want to hear, but when larger numbers of people pray, whether in a garage in Franklin, Tennessee, or in churches around the world, there always seems to be more power—even enough power to move the heart of a prideful NASCAR driver or a hardened communist.

–GC

Gracious Lord God, remind me to pray. Help me to discover the power that comes from praying with a group of like-minded believers. May my prayers bring glory to Your name. Amen.

TODAY'S READING: MATTHEW 18:19-20; ACTS 1:8,12-14; 4:23-31; 12:5-17; ROMANS 15:30-33

Prayers That Comfort

Dear brothers and sisters, I urge you in the name of our Lord Jesus Christ to join me in my struggle by praying to God for me. Do this because of your love for me, given to you by the Holy Spirit.

ROMANS 15:30

When Joey was 14, he had a brain tumor and he did not know whether he would live. Someone asked me to call him on the phone and pray for him. I did. I am sure that many people prayed for him, and it is awesome that God answered. It was fun when Joey called and said, "You prayed for me and told me if I'd keep the faith, pray and ask God to help me, I just might get out of here. Now I am racing in the Trans-Am Series."

I pray for a lot of people over the phone. Fans and people I run across know that I will do this, so when an uncle is dying of cancer or a sister has MS, someone will ask if I will call and pray. Many times I've called someone I didn't know.

Most often I never meet that person face-to-face, but sometimes I will see a person years later and he or she will say, "You prayed for my dad or my brother or my uncle, and I just want you to know it meant a lot to him."

Sometimes that person has been healed like Joey was. Other times, the person has passed away. Either way, the prayer was worth the time and effort. If God chooses to heal, prayer means everything in the world. If God chooses not to heal, at least we know we might have opened a door for that person to see God, or maybe we just gave him or her some comfort—or his or her relatives some comfort.

I host a Bible study in my garage at home for a bunch of guys. We always have a prayer time, and we make a list. If people want to see prayer answered, they need to get their prayers on our list. We've seen people healed, and we've seen people comforted. God works in many ways and He's sovereign, but this I know: Prayer may not always result in a healing, but it always comforts.

—DW

Prayer does comfort people; it is also powerful. Like DW, I have many people who ask me to pray for them. There is a bookshelf above my desk with a light underneath. Across the front of the metal box containing a long florescent bulb are 12 medium-sized yellow 3M Post-it Notes. On each are several names; 16 are scribbled on one. It's my daily prayer list.

I'm out of room on the shelf, so now if I have someone to add to my prayer list, I have to write his or her name on an existing piece of paper. Rarely does a name get removed. A person must die for that to happen. I write down just the names but not specific prayer requests. Those change, and I keep them in my head.

I mostly send up arrow prayers. Sometimes I wish I were better at praying, but I guess I don't really. If I were truly serious, I'd take steps to improve. Some people have so much to say and can think of so much to pray about. I have difficulty avoiding redundancy. After the praise-and-worship part of my prayer time, I usually ask God to take care of so-and-so today. I ask Him to meet his or her needs and remind Him to bless the person. The names are in front of me, and I pause at each one. That's the way I do it.

Margaret-Rose Macy's name was right between Al Egg and Jim Eney. Al and Jim had been there quite a while. Margaret-Rose was a more recent addition. She and her husband, Mauri, had provided music at conferences where I was the speaker. Mauri had asked me to pray. Margaret-Rose was undergoing radiation therapy.

For a long time, when I prayed for Margaret-Rose I said, "God, help Margaret-Rose. God, heal Margaret-Rose. God, give the doctors wisdom treating Margaret-Rose." Then I got the news. God had answered. Mauri sent me an address-change card with just his name on it. I cried. It was time to put a line through Margaret-Rose's name. But I added Mauri's. He's right there between Al and Jim, next to Margaret-Rose.

–GC

Most awesome God, I thank You that You care about us and that You love to talk to us—and that You like to hear back from us, too. Thank You that our prayers matter and that You hear and answer each one. Thanks, too, that sometimes the answer is no. Teach me Your ways that I might want to talk with You more and more. In Jesus' name, amen.

TODAY'S READING: HEBREWS 13:18-21; ROMANS 15:30-33; JOHN 11:17-29

On the Inside

*Then many who heard him say these things believed in him.
Jesus said to the people who believed in him, "You are truly my
disciples if you keep obeying my teachings."*

JOHN 8:30-31

I keep my hand in racing by testing cars and by driving my truck three or four times a year in the Craftsman Truck Series. There's always an element of risk, but I go slower when testing cars and I run on smaller tracks with the trucks. The odds of not wrecking are pretty good.

My brother Michael and I have a lot of fun racing the trucks. Michael and I appear in a TV commercial in which I'm begging him to let me drive his "dream machine." He's loving that.

Michael was born when I was 17 years old. The four of us who were older were out of the house for most of Michael's years at home. With his being the only one left in the house, he grew to be really close to dad. He was also a friend of the Pettys (another NASCAR family), and he was close to Dale Earnhardt. As I recounted earlier, it was Earnhardt who was blocking for Michael the day Michael won his first Winston Cup race—the Daytona 500. That was also the day Dale Earnhardt died.

I regret not having helped Michael more when he first got into racing. I was too caught up in doing my own thing. But Michael and I are close now, and I'm glad for that. He has become a believer too and is a very good person.

A lot of people think I'm Michael's dad. One time we were flying together in a private jet. I arrived first and the pilot asked, "Is your son here yet?"

Michael is funny though. Sometimes he'll go somewhere and someone will ask, "How is your dad doin'?"

He'll say, "He died."

"No, he didn't. I just saw him on TV yesterday."

It makes him mad when he goes somewhere to sign autographs and people ask, "Where's Darrell?" So he puts up a sign that reads, "I don't know where Darrell is, and he's not my dad." No wonder he will not let me drive his "dream machine." If you meet Michael and want to make him smile, ask about his older brother DW.

—DW

I hung out with DW for three days, but that didn't make me a Waltrip. Likewise, if I were to be in the pits on race day, it would not make me a crew member. I could eat ice cream at Maggie Moo's with the Waltrips or hang with the crew chief, but that will not put me in the family or on the team. All I can do is get close.

That reminds me of my days as an L.A. Laker. After a ball game, people who had enough clout were allowed into the dressing room. They wanted to get close to the players, but they weren't Lakers. There is a huge difference between being a fan and being a participant. A lot of churchgoers aren't really Christians—they only get close.

The Jews of Jesus' day were aware of their heritage. They were a chosen race and knew it. Parted waters, manna, dove, quail, rocks spouting water, floating axes, fires and spires, pillars and plagues—they had received miracles galore! They knew it, but they had become proud.

Jesus preached in the treasury inside the Temple and many people came to believe.[1] Some said, "We are Abraham's offspring."[2] They thought their heritage solved the problem of sin. Jesus said that wasn't so.[3]

The Scriptures are crystal clear on this one. The people thought they believed, but they didn't believe correctly. Their heritage kept their head knowledge from settling in their hearts.

We cannot become part of God's family by going to church, being a part of a church group, doing good deeds, living by the Golden Rule, belonging to a denomination, reciting the Lord's Prayer, claiming to be a Christian, being baptized, attending catechism, enrolling in Sunday School, memorizing Bible verses, reading the Bible, going forward for an altar call at camp or in church, being a good guy or being born in the United States.

Darrell and Michael each have a personal relationship with Jesus—they are not only Waltrips, but they are also part of God's family. This did not happen because they had Christian parents, nor did it happen because they were born in the Bible Belt. It happened because they trusted Christ and committed themselves to Him.

–*GC*

Dear Lord, I want to get this right. My faith is in Christ
and nothing else. Thank You. Amen.

TODAY'S READING: JOHN 8:21-47; GALATIANS 2:11-21;
ROMANS 10:9-10; JOHN 1:12

For Those Tears

My mom had a stroke. Stevie and I were in Dover when it occurred. She was paralyzed on her left side. She'd been going to the same doctor for 50 years; she had a hole in her heart, but he didn't know it. She would never have had this stroke if she had gone to a heart specialist.

My dad, who was as full of life as anybody you'd ever meet, loved going to the races with my brother Michael and me. He got sick with cancer and slowly died right before my eyes. I watched him go all the way down, and it was frustrating not being able to do anything about it.

The same thing happened with my father-in-law. He was one of my best friends—truly a buddy. He got cancer and died. There was nothing I could do but watch. It was a tremendous loss for me.

I had an incredible amount of respect for Bill France. He was the head of NASCAR, and he was almost as close as family. I visited him in July 2000 in Daytona at the Halifax Hospital. I walked in the room, and he was barely alive. That was tough, too. The hits just kept on coming—then Dale got killed. For a while it seemed like every time I turned around I was losing someone I cared about deeply.

I think I'm like most athletes who are well known. So many people want something from us. It's hard to know who is sincere and who isn't. I suppose that's why I don't have very many close personal friends. And I guess that's why having my mom get sick and losing so many important people in a two-year time frame was so difficult. I lost a lot in a short amount of time. It still hurts.

But the Waltrips don't cry much. We were raised with mom's motto: "Dry it up. You'll live!" That is what she would want me to do, so I try.

—DW

I walked from the United States Capitol, past the Washington Monument, to the Lincoln Memorial. After leaving a dignified Mr. Lincoln sitting and staring endlessly, I turned and accidentally came upon the Vietnam Veterans Memorial wall.

"Dear God, he was only 17," I heard one mom cry out quietly from the depth of her loss.

"Why?" came an angry demand from a dad as he stared at a name etched in stone.

"Oh, how I miss him," wailed a lonely mother.

A dad stood in silence with a sobbing daughter under each arm. He fought his feelings, but the tears racing down his cheeks showed that he'd failed. He had lost a son; he had earned his right to cry.

Brothers and sisters were there, too. Some sobbed openly. Others just whimpered. But none played—not even the little ones. The wall wasn't a place for fun. Memories of death lingered there.

People rubbed pencils over papers stretched across an etched name of a loved one, like a kid traces the surface of a coin. They would take their name home and frame it.

The memorial had a cleansing effect of finality for some. I watched a few people let go of their anger, but some could not and would never release it. All had been scarred for life. Their loved ones were gone.

I never lost anyone in Vietnam; but at the memorial, I too was scarred. I don't think I have ever felt anything like it before or since.

People who pay high prices for God and country touch me. They are worth the tears. But here, along the black-etched marble, name-stained wall, there was pain that overwhelmed loss. Such pain! I don't think I will ever be the same. The families who lost loved ones certainly are not, nor are those who survived that nightmare—or any other nightmare called war, either before or since. It was at that moment that I thought of the greatest war of all—the one fought for souls. And I wondered about the depth of sadness God must have felt when His Son died—a death so vividly portrayed in Mel Gibson's movie *The Passion of the Christ*.

Sometimes life is hard, but because Christ died for us, we can dry it up. As believers, we'll live.

–GC

Compassionate Father, comfort us when we grieve, encourage us to bear the burdens of those who hurt and help us understand the importance of the war for souls, as well as our role in the fight. Amen.

TODAY'S READING: 1 CORINTHIANS 15:54-57; EPHESIANS 6:10-13; JOB 1:20-22

The Scent of Garlic

I recall all you have done, O LORD; I remember
your wonderful deeds of long ago.

PSALM 77:11

I have lots of memories of Dale Earnhardt. He had his airplane over at a shop where I'd had mine painted. Most of the people in the shop were my fans when I was driving the Tide car. It happened that the tail number on Dale's airplane was N1DE. When he came to pick up his plane, the number had been altered. Somebody had taped over the N and put a T.

When he first saw it, he was embarrassed. Then he was so angry that he told them he'd never bring anything back there again. They were just playing, but that's how serious the competition among racers was. He did not like that joke. He could be as serious as a heart attack.

I prayed for Dale after I got serious about my faith. I didn't tell him, "I'm going to pray for you" or ask "Can I pray?" That wasn't the way to approach prayer with Dale. Sometimes I feel a need to pray for people. I don't tell them I'm praying for them and I don't ask permission. I just pray as God prompts me. Dale was one of those guys.

Right before a race, Dale and I would sometimes pray. It would often be just four of us: Dale, his wife, Stevie and me. Sometimes Max from Motor Racing Outreach or one of our chaplains joined us.

As I have recounted, Dale broke my ribs at Charlotte. I was still ticked at him as we prepared for the next race. I wasn't going to pray, but Stevie grabbed him and me and made us pray. Then she made us say "I love you" to each other. We mumbled something like "Well, yeah, I love you, man." It was enough.

Dale and I mixed friendship, envy, prayer and Scripture. It all made for an absolutely unique relationship.

–DW

I was having dinner. The antipasto salad was perfect. The Italian dressing was a house specialty. I had to shake it hard and use it quickly or I would have missed out on the goodies at the bottom. Included was a big piece of thick toasted French bread, soaked in butter and reeking of the garlic that would still be on my fingers the next morning, even though I would wash my hands.

Next came the meatball sandwich. The meatballs had been sliced, displaying the seasonings that make them unique in all of sandwichdom. The foot-and-a-half-long roll was homemade and covered with sesame seeds. The meat and the bread had been glued together with melted cheese and toasted. A steaming hot bowl of meat sauce for dipping beckoned.

My friend David Greene introduced me to the place. He is a pastor, and this restaurant is where we talked about church, families and friendship. Two years later, I was back and we talked again. Our routine has been to split the antipasto salad, the garlic bread and the sandwich.

I was here alone on this night. My friend had moved on to a different church. But I was in the neighborhood, so I stopped in and ordered what we usually ordered, an antipasto salad and a meatball sandwich. I cut the French bread in two and ate the bigger piece first. Tradition. Since David was not there, I ate both halves of the sandwich and all of the salad, too. The food was as good as ever, but it was not the same. I missed David, but I prayed for him that night. I smiled as my folded hands came to my bowed head. The scent of garlic was on my fingers.

Garlic makes me think of David Greene. The song "It Is Well with My Soul" reminds me of my friend who crashed in a plane. The start of a race makes Stevie Waltrip think about going to pit road with DW's and Dale's Scriptures. And DW often still gets a lump in his throat on the third lap of a race. In 2001, DW and Fox Sports were quiet with what they called the silent third lap in honor of Dale Earnhardt and his number three car. The fans even stood and held up three fingers. That was three years ago and the lump persists. Those are interesting memories. But our most important memory ought to be the Cross. It reminds us that we're forgiven—and that's a good time to pray and give thanks.

–*GC*

Compassionate Lord, thank You for good friends and for the joy they bring into my life. I praise You for reminders of their love. Father, bless my friends, put Your hand on them, enlarge their borders for Your sake, and keep them free from fear and harm. And thank You for Your Son. Amen.

TODAY'S READING: JOSHUA 4:1-7; JONAH 2:7; PSALM 77:11; PROVERBS 17:17; ECCLESIASTES 4:9-10; JOHN 15:12-14; 2 TIMOTHY 1:3-14

Specialists

Just as our bodies have many parts and each part has a special function, so it is with Christ's body. We are all parts of his one body, and each of us has different work to do. And since we are all one body in Christ, we belong to each other, and each of us needs all the others. God has given each of us the ability to do certain things well.

ROMANS 12:4-6

In my era, a great driver could carry a mediocre car. A driver could make up for what a car couldn't do, because there were only a few exceptional drivers. I would often tell my crew chief, "That's close enough. I'll make up the rest." And there was a time when I could do that; but not anymore.

A good driver in a great car will win a few races. A great driver in a bad car probably won't make the show. A great driver in the fastest car on the track can go into the pits leading the race, and if he has a bad pit crew, he can go out running twenty-first. He can't win the race.

To win consistently it takes three elements: driver, car and crew. The whole package is needed, and that is what teams today do differently than in my era. They have a car that will run fast, and they have a driver who knows how to win. Plus, they have a pit crew of specialists who have choreographed each move to change four tires and dump 22 gallons of gas into the car in 14 seconds. It takes a big, agile guy to work the one-pump jacks, and the man handling gas cans has to be able to accurately work with 80 pounds pressed over his head. The team rehearses each step that will be made during the pit stop.

In my day, 21 seconds for a pit stop was fast. But we used only 12 guys to do everything from working on the car to working in the pits. If we had trouble with the car during the week, the crew was exhausted by the weekend, which is when we needed them at their freshest. Today the pit crew just does the pit. When they go over the wall, they know exactly what every man is going to do and when.

Other people work on the car during the week. Teams have specialists for every aspect of the car: the suspension, gears, tires, chassis and shocks. It's just like in a medical clinic or a military unit. There is a specialist for everything.

–DW

Many book publishers were once mom-and-pop operations. Pop wrote, Mom proofread, and they hired a printer and binder. They threw some books in the backseat of their car and drove around to sell them on street corners. Now it takes a building full of specialists to get a product to various retailing establishments around the country and posted on the Internet. Editing, marketing, sales, accounting, administration, warehousing, computer support, theology experts, art and layout, printing, binding— each aspect of business requires a specialist. Mom and Pop can't get the job done anymore. These days it takes a team.

When I played for the Lakers, we had 11 guys, a coach and a trainer. Now a team can have 15 players, and there are at least six teams with a combination of eight coaches and trainers. There are position coaches, shooting coaches, coaches who specialize in offense, coaches who specialize in defense, strength and conditioning coaches and as many as three trainers. Times have changed.

In the early days of the New Testament, 12 men and Jesus did everything. In DW's racing days, 12 guys did everything, too—but when Darrell hired specialists to do the job, his pit times were almost cut in half. Forty days after Jesus died, came back to life and left like a hot air balloon that keeps on going, every Christian became a specialist and the job of making disciples became much more efficient. The Holy Spirit arrived.

No longer did the pit crew consist of 12. On Pentecost, every believer became a specialist with a job to do. On that day, and ever since, all followers of Christ were indwelled by the Holy Spirit of God. The job had become too big for the 12 disciples. There was a world to tell about Jesus. So God gave believers the power to do it.

God has given each of us as believers the ability to produce supernatural results. We get that ability when we receive Christ. And we all have our God-given natural talent from birth. God has wired each one of us to be His specialists. When our wiring is combined with instructions from God's Word and with prayer, then we're ready for service.

Have you discovered your specialty? Do you know your niche in the Body of Christ?

–GC

Lord God, You are the giver of great gifts. Thank You for empowering me with gifts, talents and the Holy Spirit. Here I am, Lord. Send me.[1] Amen.

TODAY'S READING: ACTS 2:1-13; ROMANS 12:3-8; 1 CORINTHIANS 12; EPHESIANS 4:1-16; ISAIAH 6:8

Learners Who Follow

Therefore, go and make disciples of all the nations, baptizing them in the name of the Father and the Son and the Holy Spirit. Teach these new disciples to obey all the commands I have given you. And be sure of this: I am with you always, even to the end of the age.

MATTHEW 28:19-20

There was a time when an experienced driver was an asset to a racing team. He knew what the pit crew needed to adjust to make a car hum. Nowadays that has changed. Computers produce a ton of data about the car, the track and race conditions. With printouts in their hands, the younger drivers and pit-crew members do not really care what older drivers think.

Most drivers can tell when a car isn't running right, but the younger drivers don't know how to fix it. Most older drivers, such as myself, know when something is wrong *and* what needs to be done to solve the problem.

Before the Fox broadcasts, I still roam the pits to gather information. Sometimes one of the older crew chiefs will pull me aside and ask me to test his car. Stevie doesn't care if I test a car, because she knows I'm not going to drive it as fast as it can go. I'm only going to drive it as fast as I want to go.

I am always more than happy to test a car or lend advice to a team if it gets stuck, but often my help is not wanted. My brother Michael says, "We don't do it that way anymore." I argue that I know every racetrack. When I test a car I can say, "You don't have enough right front spring for this track" or "You've got too much rebound in your rear shocks." The younger pit-crew members all look at me and say, "Huh, how'd you know that? Our driver doesn't know that stuff."

I've learned a few things over the years. I've driven off the first turn at Charlotte a million times. I know where the car's got to be, what it's got to do and how it's supposed to feel. I know the tracks and I know cars. I tell Michael all of the time, "You let me drive your car. I won't drive it as fast as you do, because it's not my car. But if you let me drive your car and let me work on it, when I say it's really good, you'll get in and be able to go really fast."

–DW

DW likes to use his knowledge and experience to help others. If he concentrated on one person, his focused help would be called mentoring. Jesus called it discipling.

The word "disciple" in Greek means "learner"[1] and in the Bible it is used to refer to the followers of Jesus. Therefore, disciples are learners who follow. Moses discipled Joshua.[2] Daniel produced Shadrach, Meshach and Abednego. (Tough names. Think *Your Shack, My Shack and a Bungalow* and you are close.) Elijah gave us Elisha.[3] Barnabas mentored John Mark.[4] And the Apostle Paul taught many disciples—I counted 23, including Titus, Timothy and the elders at Ephesus.

DW's pastor, Cortez Cooper, is his mentor. DW also disciples others. Sam Talbert is my Paul. Close to 80 people have entered into full-time Christian service for at least a time after Sam discipled them. I am one of those disciples.

I first realized he was being intentional about discipling me when he asked me to speak to some high school kids. I had just had a fight with my wife. I was mad, wasn't filled with the Spirit and really didn't want to be godly at that moment. I told him to speak instead because I didn't think that in my condition the kids would get anything out of it.

I will never forget his response: "What makes you think this evening is for the kids? It's for you. You can go in that room and pray and get filled. Or you can just go talk to the kids. Either choice will be OK with me, but if you don't go talk to those kids, I'm through with you. We'll still be friends, but I only have so much time. I want to invest it where it will have the best possible return."

Discipling, or mentoring, is serious business. We need to either be making disciples, or we need to be discipled to the point where we can make them. It's not an optional concept.[5]

Who is your Paul? To whom are you being a Paul?

–JC

Heavenly creator of life, show me if I need to be discipled, or if I should be discipling someone. Either give me a mentor, or give me someone to mentor. I will trust You to put the right person in my life. Thank You, Lord.

TODAY'S READING: MATTHEW 28:18-20; HEBREWS 5:11-14; 2 TIMOTHY 2:2; EPHESIANS 4:11-16; DEUTERONOMY 34:9; 1 KINGS 19:19; ACTS 15:39

Winning with Honor

Let us run with endurance the race that God has set before us. We do this by keeping our eyes on Jesus, on whom our faith depends from start to finish.

HEBREWS 12:1-2

Kevin Harvick was running second at Richmond and was in position to pass the front-runner to win. Just as he made his move, another driver bumped Harvick's car and slammed him into the fence. Harvick was out of the race and the driver who did the bumping finished third.

That would never have happened when I was racing. The philosophy of winning in NASCAR has changed. We went for the checkereds, but we did it honorably. Now drivers fight to finish first at any cost.

If a driver intentionally bumps another car out of the way to win or place higher in a race, NASCAR should discipline the driver who did the bumping—I think they should even take away a win. Instead, the one who was bumped is penalized.

NASCAR seems to have a policy that when the race is over, it's over. Bumping is not the only prohibited act allowed. If someone wins with an illegal engine or banned tires, he is still the winner of the race. He may be fined, but it's still a win. Because NASCAR is so reluctant to reverse results, it is incumbent upon us drivers to compete with honor.

I can only think of one time when a race result was overturned. We were racing in Nashville in 1983. Neil Bonnet passed me illegally on the last lap, and they gave him the win. I protested. A local television station had footage of the last lap of the race. The video clearly showed that Neil had violated the rules. If it hadn't been for the video, I doubt that NASCAR would have reversed the win.

All driving contracts include bonuses for wins. Some sponsors give their drivers a million-dollar bonus for winning a race. If a driver cheats and wins, he may get penalized, but he still comes out ahead because NASCAR won't take the win away. Now that is not right!

When we cheat, we may still get the checkereds and the big paycheck, but we lose part of ourselves. It is not worth the cost. I wanted to win, but I wanted to win with honor.

–DW

Some people live their lives like some of the win-at-all-costs NASCAR drivers who have little regard for the rules of the road and who never stop to count the cost. Others count the cost, race with honor and win the ultimate prize. At the end of their lives, they hear the words: "Well done."[1]

We know that David was a man after God's own heart. God said so.[2] But the man also had a big problem. The ladies!

One day the king found himself up on his rooftop and bored. A Bobby Darin song was probably blaring from a nearby boombox: "Splish splash I was takin' a bath, long about a Saturday night. A rub-dub, just relaxin' in the tub, thinkin' everything was alright."[3] There she was. Bathsheba was hot-tubbing in the buff. David checked her out. One thing led to another, sin escalated into more sin, as it usually does, and adultery led to the murder of Bathsheba's husband and the ultimate death of the son produced from D and B's union. One little sneak-a-peek resulted in a lot of hot water.

Yes, it's true that David repented and was forgiven, but think of the cost of cheating—two lives lost and nine months to two years spent away from God prior to David's confrontation with Nathan that resulted in the king's repenting. But there was another cost. God made it clear that the temple David wanted to construct to the glory of God could not be built by David because he had been a man of violence. David's sin prohibited the fulfillment of his lifelong dream and ambition. Yes, David's willingness to repent and worship made him a man after God's own heart,[4] but think how much better it could have been if he hadn't cheated.

God forgives our sin, but He doesn't fix the consequences. We have to live with those. I've done enough in my life to-date that is embarrassing and my sinfulness has no doubt limited my usefulness for the Kingdom. Since sin always has lasting consequences, I don't want to limit what's left of my usefulness and I don't want to be embarrassed at the end. I want to run what's left of my race with honor. I want to hear a big, loud "Well done!" How about you?

–GC

Almighty God, I want to fulfill all the plans You have for me. I don't want sin to restrict what You would have me do. With all my heart I want to honor You with my life, and I would like to honor You when it's my time to die. Amen.

TODAY'S READING: MATTHEW 24:14-30; HEBREWS 12:1-13; 1 CHRONICLES 28:2-3; 1 SAMUEL 13:13-14; PROVERBS 21:21; 22:4; 2 CORINTHIANS 13:7

Champions

Therefore, since we are surrounded by such a huge crowd of witnesses to the life of faith, let us strip off every weight that slows us down, especially the sin that so easily hinders our progress. And let us run with endurance the race that God has set before us.

HEBREWS 12:1

The young guys are all adrenaline—they're all about having no fear. They just drive the wheels off the car. Their attitude is, "If I wreck, I wreck!" The thing that makes young guys hard to beat is they go all out all the time. They drive every lap like they are trying to qualify. That's not a smart way to drive, but sometimes these young drivers make it—and if they make it, they beat you.

For some drivers, winning races is more important than winning the championship. But the championship is everything. Week-to-week racing is one thing, but championship racing is big-picture racing. Week-to-week racing is trying to win every individual race. When you try to do that, you do not last and you are not around for the championship.

Here's the big picture: I want to win the championship, so I've got 36 races in which to do it. I've got to start every race, and I've got to do everything I can to finish every race. I can't crash and I can't blow up. Since I run 400 to 500 miles every week and I am out on the track three and a half hours, conditioning, saving a little something for the stretch run, and keeping the car intact are important. Each of those things is going to earn me points. And points win championships.

When I was a racer, I would start at Daytona in February. Everybody has a clean sheet of paper at that point. It's the first race of the year, but our biggest race. It is our Super Bowl.

Some guys go to win the Daytona 500. Other guys go to start their season-long battle to win the championship. When a racer starts running the race, there are two ways to approach it. He can run to win that race or he can run to be around and win the championship at the end of the year. Jeff Gordon is the only young guy who started off his career winning championships. All the rest of the champions won most of theirs after they turned 30. I won 84 races; I was in the position to win 10 championships, but I only won 3.

–DW

There are two ways to run a race: the old way and the new way. The old way is the Old Covenant (or Old Testament). If you race this way, you have to win every time out, and you could be in big trouble if you don't. This is sometimes called legalism. It's living under the Law, and for the most part, living under the oppression of those who interpret the Law. The Ten Commandments were given to show us that we can't live up to them, that we can't win every race and that we need a different way to race if we are going to win the championship prize, which is a place in heaven.

The new way to run the race of faith is the New Covenant (or New Testament). The New Covenant is all about depending on Christ and the Holy Spirit. God only spoke to a few people during the Old Covenant. But He speaks heart-to-heart with each of us in the New Covenant.

No one has ever won all the Winston Cup races in a single season. Half is the best so far. Richard Petty and Jeff Gordon each did it once but in different eras. I suppose someone might win them all someday, but it is unlikely. There are too many variables. No one has ever kept the whole Law either. Like the unlikelihood of winning all the races, the Bible makes it clear that no one is capable of keeping the whole Law.

Try as we might, we will never get into heaven on our own merit. The Old Covenant required us to be perfect. Only Jesus lived a perfect life. The New Covenant requires us to put our trust in Jesus' perfect life. The first is impossible. The second sets us free.

Jesus is the key to the championship.

–GC

Holy God of grace, thank You for freeing me from the Law and for sending Your Son to pay the price for my failures. I place my trust in Him and Him alone. Amen.

TODAY'S READING: ECCLESIASTES 9:11; HEBREWS 12:1; 18-24; PHILIPPIANS 2:16

The Eyes Have It

Clearly, you are a letter from Christ prepared by us. It is written not with pen and ink, but with the Spirit of the living God. It is carved not on stone, but on human hearts.

2 CORINTHIANS 3:3

When I first meet someone, I do not ask, "Are you a Christian?" I simply put out my hand and I shake theirs. That's the connection. I can tell a lot by a handshake and a look in the eye.

Christians want to connect with each other. In that way, we are a bit like NASCAR fans. Just mention a race and NASCAR fans light up: "Oh, are you a fan? I am, too. Boogity, boogity, boogity!" Just mention the name Jesus and Christians light up. At some point we can ask each other, "Oh, you must be a Christian, too?" But usually we will be sure of the answer before it is given.

When I start talking to somebody, I don't want to have to say, "I'm a Christian." I like it best when the person knows by the way I act and talk, and by who I am. It bothers me when I have to tell somebody, "Hey, I'm a believer." I want the person to say, "You're a Christian, aren't you? I could tell." If he or she cannot tell, it may mean I am doing something wrong. If he or she can tell, it means the Holy Spirit is talking and I'm doing something right.

When I lead others to Christ, I make sure that they know God's not going to immediately fix all of their problems. This is just the beginning. With God, they have got somewhere to take their problems. They don't have to carry them on their shoulders or bury them inside.

I don't argue with people about Jesus. I don't try to convince anyone. I don't have a method. I just have a soft heart. If somebody wants Jesus, I'm more than happy to be the instrument to make it happen. Jesus is my friend. I am not ashamed to talk to people about Him.

If I am doing things right, a nonbeliever will see Him in me and will ask, "You are a Christian, aren't you?" When I meet another Christian, we will know by the handshake, the look in our eyes, the way we act and the common spirit that connects us.

—DW

With a look and a word Jesus collected His disciples. It must have been a great look. If He had walked around Santa Barbara instead of Galilee, it might have gone something like this:

I have a new friend. He hasn't been in town long. This guy has some kind of eyes but no tact. A lot of people do not like him much because of what they see as intolerance in him. It's true, he's not politically correct; but people would hang with him if they would just look into his eyes.

At first glance, he might look like a hypocrite. Sometimes late at night he can be found downtown on State Street. He rubs shoulders with the crowd on Haley, too. That freaks me out—definitely not my style. A person could get cut or catch something there. But he hangs with the people there, touches them and even holds the homeless. I keep telling him, "Those people have crawling things on them, and worse!" That doesn't seem to faze him a bit. He sticks with them and asks them to look deeply into his eyes.

My friend knows his Bible. I've never seen anything like it. He has even debated professors at a local Christian college and caused quite a stir. The professors were mad because of their loss of face more than a failure in protocol. None of them looked into his eyes.

He's asked me to go with Him on road trips. I keep waiting for him to ask, "Would you give up Santa Barbara for Bakersfield? For Barstow?" I don't know. I love it on the Central Coast. Besides, it's scary to be with him. Sometimes the crowds get out of control. One of these days, someone's going to punch him or worse. Whoever is with him might get hurt, too.

I guess I need to fish or cut bait, but it's a hard decision. I like to be liked and not punched, and I like it where I live. But I've looked into His eyes. And I catch myself wondering, Who do people see when they look into my eyes?

–*JC*

Heavenly provider of eternal life, thank You for glimpses of eternity through the eyes of Your Son in whom we have eternal life. Give us the courage to show Jesus to our friends and to follow Him. Amen.

TODAY'S READING: JOHN 1:13; 2 PETER 3:18; ISAIAH 61:10;
MATTHEW 5:16; 7:24

All in the family. Leroy and Margaret Waltrip were huge supporters of their son's dream of becoming a race-car driver. They joined DW and Stevie (above) at the races as often as possible. So did Stevie's parents, Leticia and Frank Rader (right). In 1996, Darrell celebrates with his brother Michael, who had just won a Winston Cup race (below).

Lots of fun. Whether behind the wheel of a faux race car (right) or at Maggie Moos (below), the Waltrips know how to have a good time. You think DW takes racing seriously, just look at him when it comes to protecting his ice cream! And, obviously, daughters Jessica and Sarah both have the Waltrip family know-how-to-laugh gene.

ENDNOTES

INTRODUCTION
1. Chris Ballard, "The Boogity Man," *Sports Illustrated* (December 1, 2002), p. 78.

DAY 2
1. See Acts 5:3-4.
2. See Acts 5:9.

DAY 3
1. 2 Samuel 22:3.

DAY 4
1. See Proverbs 27:17.
2. See Genesis 37:34.
3. See John 11:35-36.
4. See Acts 8:2.

DAY 5
1. See Exodus 23:14-17.
2. See Nehemiah 8:2.

DAY 6
1. Wayne Cordeiro, *Dream Releasers* (Ventura, CA: Regal Books, 2002), p. 37.
2. See John Bradley and Jay Carty, *Discovering Your Natural Talents: How to Love What You Do and Do What You Love* (Colorado Springs, CO: NavPress, 1994).

DAY 7
1. Matthew 26:34,75.
2. See Matthew 26:35.
3. See Matthew 26:69-75.
4. Matthew 26:70.
5. Matthew 26:72.
6. See Matthew 26:73-74.
7. See Luke 22:31.
8. See Acts 2:41.
9. See Acts 4:4.
10. See Acts 4:3.

DAY 8

1. See Romans 7:24.

DAY 10

1. See Acts 9:1-31.
2. See 2 Corinthians 11:23-28.

DAY 11

1. See Romans 12:3.
2. See James 1:21.
3. See Romans 12:10.
4. See Matthew 18:3-4.
5. See Psalm 25:9.

DAY 13

1. See Matthew 28:19-20.
2. See Hebrews 10:25.
3. See Matthew 7:22-23.
4. Matthew 25:21.

DAY 14

1. Matthew 23:13-29.

DAY 15

1. See Genesis 2:1-3.
2. See Leviticus 25:2-7.
3. See Judges 14:12,17.
4. See Genesis 41:1-36.
5. See Genesis 29:15-30.
6. See Revelation 2—3.
7. See Matthew 18:21.
8. See Leviticus 25:8-55.
9. See Exodus 24:1,9.
10. See Jeremiah 25:12; 29:10.
11. See Daniel 9:24.
12. See Luke 10:1-17.
13. See Matthew 18:22.

DAY 16

1. Fran Striker, "The Lone Ranger Creed," *The Celebrity Hosting Network*. http://www.celebhost.net/claytonmoore/creed.html (accessed February 2, 2004).
2. See Proverbs 18:24.

3. See 2 Thessalonians 3:10.
4. See 2 John 1:2.

Day 17
1. See Psalm 51:10-13.

Day 19
1. See Matthew 21:12-13.
2. See Matthew 22:37.

Day 22
1. See 1 Kings 18:4.
2. 2 Kings 1:8.
3. See 1 Kings 17:10-11.
4. Author unknown (probably Josephus).
5. See 1 Kings 17:13.
6. See 1 Kings 17:15.

Day 23
1. Josh McDowell, *Evidence That Demands a Verdict, Volume 1* (San Bernardino, CA: Here's Life Publishers, n.d.), n.p.

Day 25
1. See Ephesians 5:25.
2. Psalm 139:23-24, *NIV*.

Day 27
1. See Numbers 16:1-33.

Day 29
1. See 1 Corinthians 2:1-5.
2. See Acts 3:8.
3. See Deuteronomy 4:2; Revelation 22:18-19; Proverbs 30:6.

Day 30
1. See Job 1:21-22.

Day 31
1. See Joshua 24:15.

DAY 32

1. A concept I learned while speaking at a church on the Ute reservation near Durango, Colorado.

DAY 34

1. Marty Smith, "Television Deal to Reach Broader Audience in '02," Turner Sports Interactive (January 24, 2002).
2. See Nehemiah 6:15.
3. Nehemiah 6:3.
4. Lee Iacocca quoted at "*The Motivational and Inspirational Corner*," *Power Performance*. http://www.motivational-inspirational-corner.com/getquote. html?startrow=11&categoryid=59 (accessed January 8, 2004).

DAY 36

1. Matthew 4:10.

DAY 37

1. See 1 Corinthians 8:13.
2. See Exodus 3—4; Numbers 9:13.

DAY 38

1. See Acts 14:12.
2. See Romans 6:1, *KJV, NASB*.
3. Philippians 3:8.
4. Ephesians 4:26.

DAY 40

1. Matthew 6:14.

DAY 41

1. See John 4:5-26.
2. See Matthew 9:9-13.
3. Matthew 9:10, *NASB*.

DAY 42

1. James 1:4, *NASB*.

DAY 43

1. Matthew 16:15.
2. Matthew 16:16.
3. Matthew 16:18.

DAY 46

1. See Revelation 20:12.

DAY 48

1. United Press International, "Study: Red Sea Parting Was Possible," January 22, 2004. washingtontimes.com, http://washingtontimes.com/upi-breaking/20040121-080423-3978r.htm (accessed January 22, 2004).

DAY 50

1. Bob Sjogren, "Lecture One: Introducing Dog and Cat Theology," http://www.gospelcom.net/unveilinglory/Cat%20and%20Dog%20Theology%20Seminar%20Notes.pdf (access date not available).

DAY 51

1. Ioan Teodosiu's story was originally reported by Christian Solidarity International and various media outlets. The editors of this book verified the facts during a January 2004 telephone conversation with Ligia Teodosiu.

DAY 53

1. See John 8:30.
2. See John 8:33.
3. See John 8:44.

DAY 56

1. See Isaiah 6:8.

DAY 57

1. *New Unger's Bible Dictionary*.
2. See Numbers 11:28.
3. See 1 Kings 19:19.
4. See Acts 15:39.
5. See Matthew 28:18-20.

DAY 58

1. See Matthew 25:21.
2. See 1 Chronicles 28:2-3.
3. Bobby Darin, "Splish Splash," http://www.lyricsxp.com/lyrics/s/splish_splash_bobby_darin.html (accessed March 3, 2004).
4. See 1 Samuel 13:14; Acts 13:22.

It all started with go-kart racing trophies.

DARRELL WALTRIP'S RECORD AND AWARDS

Bill France Award of Excellence—2000
NASCAR Winston Cup Champion—1981, 1982, 1985
Most Popular Driver Award—1989, 1990
NASCAR Winston Cup Illustrated Person of the Year—1997
American Driver of the Year—1979, 1981, 1982
NASCAR Driver of the Decade—1980s
National Motorsports Press Association Driver of the Year—
1977, 1981, 1982
Auto Racing Digest Driver of the Year—1981, 1982
Tennessee Professional Athlete of the Year—1979

CAREER HIGHLIGHTS AND TOTALS

84 NASCAR Winston Cup victories: tied for third with Bobby Allison on all-time list.

37 Superspeedway victories: seventh on all-time list.

59 Winston Cup poles: fourth on all-time list.

23 Superspeedway poles: tied for sixth with Bobby Allison on all-time list.

Won 1989 Daytona 500.

Only driver to win $500,000 or more in a season 18 times.

Only five-time winner of the Coca-Cola 600 (1978, 1979, 1985, 1988 and 1989) at Charlotte Motor Speedway.

Won inaugural The Winston at Charlotte in 1985.

Won modern era record of 8 races from pole in 1981; tied all-time record of 4 straight.

Won 7 of 10 short-track races in 1982; shares record.

Won 1981 Busch Clash.

First Winston Cup driver to earn $10 million (February 18, 1990).
NASCAR Busch Grand National Series 13 wins
American Speed Association 7 wins
International Race of Champions 3 wins
Automobile Racing Club of America 2 wins
NASCAR All-American Challenge Series 2 wins
All Pro Racing Association 2 wins
United States Auto Club 1 win
ARTGO Challenge Series 1 win

Driver of the Decade. DW was named the best in the 1980s. Here Dale Earnhardt, Sr., James Garner and Cale Yarborough celebrate with Darrell in Los Angeles.

Winston Cup Champion.
DW won NASCAR's most coveted award in 1981, 1982 (above, with DW's parents) and 1985 (right).

First families. Darrell, Stevie and Jessica visit President George Bush and First Lady Barbara Bush at the White House in 1989 (above). NASCAR CEO Bill France and his wife, Betty, were there, too. The entire Waltrip family hangs out with George W. Bush (below).

ABOUT JAY CARTY

I knew I was a good speaker. For 27 years I spoke in churches, youth camps and other Christian venues—then I lost my voice. Frankly, I was always a little surprised that God didn't give me a greater profile. Standing 6-feet, 8-inches, I was certainly one of the tallest people behind any pulpit, though many are larger in girth. But here I do not infer physical size; rather, I mean sphere of influence.

Among Christian speakers, there are eagles, falcons, hawks and buzzards. Billy Graham, Charles Colson and James Dobson are eagles. I was a buzzard. Nonetheless, sometimes I would catch myself thinking *I'm a better communicator than so-and-so, but he's doing big gigs and I'm in little churches. What's going on God?*

That's when I came to realize that my responsibility to God is a vertical relationship. His responsibility is horizontal influence. And God chose to limit and then stop my impact as a speaker, a vocation in which I suppose I was more reliant on my natural ability than I was on God.

When I could no longer speak before crowds, God thrust me out of my comfort zone and into a place where I am totally dependent on Him. He opened the door for the One-on-One series of books, even though I was not a trained writer. That was a huge step for a kid who grew up in the Mojave Desert of California.

GROWING UP

As a kid I didn't know Jesus as my Savior, but I began to trust God. I could pray, "Now I lay me down to sleep" and I would call out to God to help me get through the night when my parents were fighting or were drunk again.

When I was in the third grade, a family from down the street convinced my mom and me to go to church one night. There was an invitation and my mom asked me if I would go forward. I thought she wanted to go, so I went with her. She went to get me saved. Neither of us was, but we each went for the other.

Because of my parents' drinking and fighting, we moved a lot. When I entred a new school at the start of the fourth grade, my teacher was worried about my development, thinking that being so much taller than everyone else would be bad for me. As a remedy, I was placed in front of the fifth grade class and was told to read three paragraphs from a book. I knew how to read, so the teacher was impressed and the next day I was in the fifth grade.

Early in junior high, my mom gave me a *King James Bible*. I enjoyed reading the Old Testament stories and looking up the naughty words. I always thought I was getting away with something when I read the word "bastard." It actually appears twice.

I was in the seventh grade when my folks finally divorced. At this writing, I am 62 and it still hurts.

Dad was a bookie. That's a person who illegally takes bets on horse races. He also ran the poker games in the back of a bar. I was a bar kid and became an expert shuffleboard player on the old, long wooden tables with the round metal pucks that I learned to accurately lag with either hand. An old alcoholic named Bill and I never lost a game. He would get a beer and I would get a Coke.

I knew what my dad did was illegal, so one day after school I confronted him. I was the one who cleaned the bookie joint on Saturday, and I didn't want to be a part of an illegal activity. I told him that I wasn't proud of what he did, and I asked him to stop and do the right thing instead. I approached him on Friday and he sold out on Monday, started a legitimate business and retired ten years later with a car dealership. He even married the woman with whom he had been living. I was proud of my dad and was grateful to God.

When I was 14, I went forward during an altar call at an old-fashioned style revival meeting and received Jesus Christ as my Savior for real.

FROM BASKETBALL TO BOOKS

I played and coached basketball at Oregon State University. I also assisted Coach John Wooden for three years at UCLA while I worked on my doctorate. And I played a year for the Los Angeles Lakers.

After my basketball playing days were over, I spent five years in business and eventually went into Christian ministry. I ran a Christian camp, was a church consultant and directed Yes! Ministries. In May 2002, I contracted a paralyzed vocal cord, ceased public speaking, stopped traveling and sought God for direction and healing. That is when an unexpected door

Jay and Mary Carty

opened: I cowrote the bestselling *Coach Wooden One-on-One* while I waited upon God. And, I have now cowritten *Darrell Waltrip One-on-One*.

I am no longer anxious for healing. I'd rather stay home, write and hang out with my wife.

FOR MORE INFORMATION

DARRELL WALTRIP

Darrell Waltrip Motorsports
P.O. Box 381
Harrisburg, NC 28075

www.dwstore.com
www.allwaltrip.com

JAY CARTY

1033 Newton Road
Santa Barbara, CA 93103

www.jaycarty.com
jay@jaycarty.com

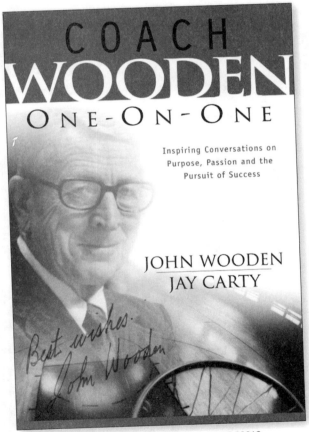

Check Out These Other Best-Sellers

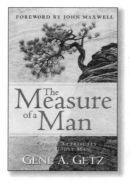

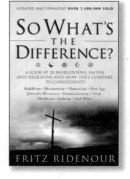